Ancient Magick for
Today's Witch Series

PROTECTION MAGICK

MONIQUE JOINER SIEDLAK

oshunpublications.com

Protection Magick © Copyright 2019 Monique Joiner Siedlak

ISBN 978-1-950378-24-1 (Paperback)

ISBN 978-1-961362-21-5 (Hardback)

ISBN 978-1-950378-23-4 (eBook)

All rights reserved

The content contained within this book may not be reproduced, duplicated or transmitted without direct written permission from the author or the publisher.

Under no circumstances will any blame or legal responsibility be held against the publisher, or author, for any damages, reparation, or monetary loss due to the information contained within this book, either directly or indirectly.

Legal Notice

This book is copyright protected. It is only for personal use. You cannot amend, distribute, sell, use, quote or paraphrase any part, or the content within this book, without the consent of the author or publisher.

Disclaimer Notice

Please note the information contained within this document is for educational and entertainment purposes only. All effort has been executed to present accurate, up to date, reliable, complete information. No warranties of any kind are declared or implied. Readers acknowledge that the author is not engaged in the rendering of legal, financial, medical or professional advice. The content within this book has been derived from various sources. Please consult a licensed professional before attempting any techniques outlined in this book.

By reading this document, the reader agrees that under no circumstances is the author responsible for any losses, direct or indirect, that are incurred as a result of the use of the information contained within this document, including, but not limited to, errors, omissions, or inaccuracies.

Cover Design by MJS

Cover Images by MidJourney

Published by Oshun Publications

www.oshunpublications.com

ANCIENT MAGICK FOR TODAY'S WITCH SERIES

The *Ancient Magick for Today's Witch Series* is a series for modern witches to explore ancient magick, covering Celtic, Gypsy, and Crystal magic, among others. It offers practical advice on spells, rituals, and enchantments for today's use, incorporating natural energies and spiritual connections. With insights into Shamanism, Wicca, and more, it helps readers enhance their magickal journey, offering paths to protection, prosperity, and spiritual growth by combining ancient wisdom with contemporary practice.

Wiccan Basics

Candle Magick

Wiccan Spells

Love Spells

Abundance Spells

Herb Magick

Moon Magick

Creating Your Own Spells

Gypsy Magic

Protection Magick

Celtic Magick

Shamanic Magick

Crystal Magic

Sacred Spaces

Solitary Witchcraft

Novice Witch's Guide

MONIQUE JOINER SIEDLAK

GET UPDATES, FREEBIES & GIVEAWAYS

JOIN MY NEWSLETTER

MOJOSIEDLAK.COM/MOONLIGHT-MUSINGS

CONTENTS

What Is Wiccan Protection	xiii
1. Why You Need Protection	1
2. Introduction to Spells	7
3. When Do You Need Protection?	13
4. Casting a Circle	19
5. Working Without a Circle	25
6. Your Altar	31
7. Objects of Protection	37
8. Personal Protection	43
9. Protection for Your Home	49
10. Recognizing Attacks	55
11. Guardian Angels	61
12. Counter-Magick	67
13. Reversal Magick	75
14. Cleanse Your Space	83
15. Psychic Attack	89
Conclusion	95
References	99
About the Author	101
More Books by Monique	103
Don't Miss Out	107

WHAT IS WICCAN PROTECTION

The world can be a beautiful place, but it can also be a dangerous one. There's a lot out there to wear us down, whether that's spiritually, emotionally, mentally, or physically. When we let the negativity in our lives begin to overwhelm our happiness, the build-up of bad energy around us becomes more and more challenging to overcome.

Worse, it's not always natural rhythms that put us in harm's way. Sometimes we can come under attack from someone else's negative energies or wishes. Harmful thoughts or even situations that we believe to be just "bad luck" are sometimes an indicator that there is a toxic person in our environment. This may be the person who is introducing negative energy through their poisonously evil wishes.

In Wicca, protection spells and rituals are like preventative medicine — they're ritualistic and energetic steps we can take to keep negative energy away from us. Unlike clearing or cleansing magick, which is all about freeing us from the negative build-up that's already around us, protection magick is about preventing that build-up from happening in the first place. There are several ways to engage with protective magick, including spellwork, amulets and talismans, color magick, and working with specific crystals or stones.

This book will take you through the ins and outs of Wiccan protection magick. This book will include plenty of spells and rituals, as well as the ideal astrological times to perform each spell. For those of you who are brand spanking new to Wicca, don't worry! This book will include an essential guide to what spells are, how they work, and how protective spells typically differ from other kinds of ritual work. Most Wiccan traditions use circles when casting spells, so if you're new to Wiccan spellwork, there is a chapter for you on how to cast a circle. However, if you belong to a neo-pagan tradition that doesn't use circles or if circles aren't part of your practice, there is a chapter for you how to cast spells without the use of a circle safely.

Protection magick is preventative, and this makes it slightly different from other kinds of magick. To properly protect yourself, you shouldn't wait to cast protective spells after you're already in danger. This book will include a guide on how to optimize your altar for energetic protection and how to use protective symbols, one of the oldest forms of protective magick we have. It will also guide you through working with angels as protective guardians and teach you how to guard yourself against the evil eye.

This book will give you strategies, spells, and symbols for protecting both yourself and your home. With a little adjustment, many of the home protection strategies can be altered to protect your workplace or other spaces where you spend a great deal of time. Negative energies can attach themselves to our person, but these energies can also be inherited from the environment. It's especially important to be careful when entering a new space. You can't always be sure what kind of energy was left over from the previous occupant.

Unfortunately, sometimes, the negative energy coming at us is stronger than our normal defenses. In this case, we need to do some clearing or cleansing work to banish the negative forces that have invaded our lives and return to a place of spiritual wellness. For that reason, this book will include a small section on cleansing magick. Not to mention, a guide on what psychic attacks are and how you can recognize when you're being targeted.

You'll notice that some of the spells in this book seem lighthearted and contemporary, while others seem more solemn and old-fashioned. Some are straightforward, while others ask for a bit more preparation. That's as it should be, as the spells in this book will be a mix of new, contemporary magick and traditional spellwork. The spells in this book come from a variety of pagan traditions and appeal to practitioners from all different backgrounds. Spells with more contemporary language or lighthearted spellwork are not meant to be taken as a joke. They are intended to make the user feel more relaxed and connected to the work they are doing. All spellwork should begin with intention and care. The energy that you send out into the universe during a spell is far more powerful than you may even realize. In spite of that, it doesn't mean it always has to feel solemn and serious. The wide variety of spells and strategies provided in this book is intended to give you the independence to pick and determine what works for you and what doesn't. Some spells may seem right at this moment but won't feel right later on and vice versa. Give yourself the freedom to engage with the protective strategies that feel right for you and leave the ones that don't speak to you at this moment. In the future, you can always come back to this book for some extra guidance.

The spells in this book will also be accompanied by the ideal astrological time at which the spell should be completed. This process will often have to do with the phase or position of the sun or moon. However, this could refer to other planets as well. In the introduction to spellwork, there will be a brief guide on how to determine which planets are in which astrological houses. There are recommendations for how to check and follow the phases of the moon. While protection magick is appropriate all year round, the nature of the spells is more powerful at different times of the year. These spells will engage with different energies present in the planet's natural rhythms.

This book has been written with the assumption that readers live in the northern hemisphere, but if this is not true for you, simply reverse the seasonal recommendations. For example, if a spell is more potent in the summer or winter, adjust the monthly references to coincide with the summer and winter as it occurs in your hemisphere.

Protection magick is like energetic malware protection — it puts active shields in place so that you can continue to live and grow in the peace that you deserve. This makes protection magick some of the most basic and important magick we can incorporate into our practice, but it also makes it some of the least exciting. Unlike other spells or rituals, you know that a protection spell is working when nothing happens! No matter what spellwork you do, it's always tempting to wait anxiously to see the results. It is part of our human nature. We want to harvest the fruits of our labor. However, protection magick is a bit more subtle and requires a bit more patience. Again, if life is relatively uneventful in the months after a protection spell, that's actually the best sign that your spell is working. The best way to enjoy the benefits of protective magick is to adopt a mindset of gratitude. Don't waste time and energy, waiting to see the results of your spells. The greatest gift we get from engaging in protective rituals is the accompanying adjustment of perspective. After protective measures are put in place, we have a new appreciation for our safety and comfort. We naturally begin looking for the things that are going right rather than at what is going wrong. We want to see that our spells are working after all!

Whether you are entirely new to Wiccan spellwork or have been practicing for years, this book will pass on that gift to you. The rituals in this book are accessible for people of all traditions and ability levels and can be modified with small adjustments to fit the individual needs of every practitioner. The only tools you need to engage in successful protective rituals are patience and a little practice. Whether you are under a vicious psychic attack or you want to feel a bit more energetically secure, this book has something for you.

1
WHY YOU NEED PROTECTION

You believe that, for the most part, the world's natural energies are positive and good. You do what you can to bring positivity into the lives of others. Therefore, you can expect them to give positivity back. You do regular cleanses, you don't rely too much on luck to achieve your goals, and you have a dedicated altar space. Do you really need protection?

The simple answer is yes. The energies around us are complex. It's hard to categorize our energetic environments, as in all respects, completely positive or negative. Different people want different things. Different people require different things, and sometimes those energies can come into conflict with each other. Worse, people don't always understand how to communicate or achieve their needs in a healthy way. One moment of pain or deprivation can turn into toxic emotional habits that can be incredibly dangerous to anyone exposed to them. Yes, you might be doing a great deal to bring positive energy into the spaces around you, but you don't always necessarily get what you give. You aren't the only influence on the lives and emotions of the people around you. Someone immersed in negativity might be pushing much stronger negative influences at you than you even realize. Those around us who are deeply unhappy or unhealthy can exude a powerful negative impact. If we aren't properly protecting ourselves, then we will get caught up in their negative narratives instead of helping them to grow or heal. If you don't have protective measures in place, you can easily get caught in the toxic intentions of those around you.

We know that places can also hold energy. If you are moving into a new place, starting a new job, or staying for a short time in a hotel, you don't know what energies may be lingering there from the previous inhabitants. These energies go for dormitories or other temporary living space.

Cleansing rituals are great for moving into new spaces. The only thing, you can't always sage your office or do a cleansing spell in the college dorm room you share with two other people. Protective talismans, spells, and altar spaces help to protect you from the unexpected or residual energies you encounter on a daily basis. They can keep you safe no matter where you go. Negative energies can deeply attach themselves to a location. If you aren't protected, you may not even realize that you are tangled up in those energies until it's too late. Worse, you can start bringing those energies from their place of origin into other safe spaces in your life.

Sometimes it's not an accident when you come under negative influences. People can outright psychically attack us, and if we aren't suitably protected, we can be very vulnerable indeed to the ill wishes of others. Again, we know that giving out positive energy goes a long way toward bringing it back to us. Sometimes the intense negative energy hurled at us is much stronger than the gentle, positive energies we emanate to those around us. Persistent psychic attacks are much more powerful than the poisonous negative energy of a deeply unhappy or unhealthy person. It can even break through our basic defenses if we aren't aware of their negative influences. Everybody needs the protection of some kind. Simply because you can't be sure what's out there every time you leave (or allow someone else to enter) your home.

Our ancestors were well conscious of the dangers around them, both in the physical world and on the spiritual plane. This is why protective magick is some of the oldest magick we know and is universal to all ancient cultures around the globe. Charms, amulets, talismans, and other protective symbols are found across the world and survive in every significant religion active in the world today. Christians often wear crosses to protect themselves from evil influences, and Catholics will sometimes wear medals to appeal to the protective powers of various saints. Jews of many denominations hang a mezuzah on their doorpost to protect the inhabitants from harmful external influences. Mediterranean cultures wear various talismans and charms to protect themselves from the evil eye. The most culturally recognizable being the hamsa and the blue eye talisman worn in Turkey and Greece. Italians hang a red horn from the rearview mirrors in their cars to protect against the evil eye. Chinese men and women wear jade bracelets, necklaces, and amulets to protect themselves from spirits and negative energies.

Protective symbols, rituals, and even patterns of dress are found in cultures across the African continent. Indigenous people of the American southwest wore turquoise jewelry to release negative energies and protect themselves from harmful external influences. You may have hung a dream catcher in your room as a child to protect yourself from evil spirits at night.

All of this scratches the surface of the ways humans have been spiritually protecting themselves for thousands of years. Whether it's as simple as a protective talisman or as elaborate as an entire cleansing ritual, you'll learn protection magick is integral to keeping ourselves safe from unwanted psycho-spiritual influences that harm our spirit. It can even manifest as mental or physical illness. In neo-pagan and Wiccan traditions, we attempt to take the ancient wisdom of our ancestors (wherever they may have come from) and apply their spiritual knowledge in a way that makes sense for the contemporary world.

In many ways, we are exposed to psychic and supernatural threats that our ancestors never dreamed of before. In the contemporary world, not only do we have to worry about the psychic residue we encounter in physical spaces, but we also have to contend with the psychic energies present in digital spaces. In other ways, we are facing the same risks that we have been encountering as a species since the time of old.

No matter what your spiritual tradition or which neo-pagan path you follow, protection magick is an essential piece of your spiritual practice. As someone who works with spells, energies, and auras daily, you are opening yourself up to spiritual and psychic influences more often than people who follow different spiritual paths. When you engage in spellwork, you aren't just sending your own energy out into the universe. You are also exposing yourself to the more profound and more powerful energies that are flowing around you. For this reason, it is especially important as a pagan or earth-based practitioner that you know how to protect yourself. Protection magick ensures that you don't attract unwanted psychic attacks or get caught in psychic flows of energy that are too powerful for you to control. You need protective magick for the same reason that your front door needs a lock. You aren't expecting someone to break into your home when you lock the door at night. It's a precautionary measure. Just in case something happens, you know you can rest easy when you go to sleep at night.

Think of protective magick as a spiritual lock, an energetic protective shield that keeps all but the most intense psychic attacks at bay. You need protective magick not because you are expecting an attack but for the peace of mind that comes with knowing that your spirit is safe and secure as you grow and thrive in this energetically complicated world.

2

INTRODUCTION TO SPELLS

Spellwork is the ceremonial heart of the Wiccan practice. As such, there are many protective spells that you can use to keep yourself and your space free from danger. If you're new to Wicca or witchcraft, however, diving straight into working with spells can be a bit intimidating. Like anything, spellwork takes practice to perfect. But not to worry!

The best time to begin is now, and protective spells, in particular, are very accessible to beginners and advanced practitioners alike. The most common experience new practitioners have when they begin spellwork is ... well, nothing.

You cast your spell, you follow the steps, you copy everything out of the spellbook or off the internet perfectly, and nothing changes. This is a frustrating experience that all of us go through in the beginning, and the only way through it is patience. With protective magick, however, nothing is exactly what you want!

Remember, protection spells are some of the most ancient and elemental we have. Consequently, protective magick is not nearly as complicated or energetically taxing as other kinds of magick.

This chapter will give you a small introduction to what spells are, how they work so that you can dive right in and start practicing with the individual spells that are outlined for you later in this book.

Knowing how spells work will also help you to understand how more uncomplicated protective measures like stones, amulets, and charms work as well.

In a way, wearing a protective amulet is one of the most basic spells you can cast. Having this understanding in your mind will help you to apply protective symbols to your spellwork and overall practice. It will also help you to optimize your altar space with small protective measures to keep your sacred space safe from invasion.

Even if you aren't strictly Wiccan, most neo-pagan and earth-worshiping traditions use spellwork in one form or another. It's the casting of spells that makes our spirituality a "craft" rather than a religion. Rather than passively accepting the flow of energy around us or petitioning more powerful entities to act on our behalf, we harness the power to alter and contribute to those energetic flows with intention, to gain the results that will most benefit us. This doesn't always manifest in the ways that we expect, and often, spellwork goes a long way toward teaching us about who we are and what we want.

The only distinctive talent or skill that spellwork requires of you is visualization. Spellwork is an exercise in imagination. If imagining is something you have trouble with, then you'll need a bit more practice to start seeing results when you start casting.

Visualization is simply the ability to see something in your mind that isn't there before you in real life. Picture your friend's face. Picture a flag waving in the breeze. Picture what your street looks like in the fall. Can you do it? Then you already have the ability to visualize!

What Is a Spell?

So what exactly is a spell? In the simplest terms, a spell is a redirection of psychic energy with the purpose of realizing an intention. In other words, you want something, and then you take ritualistic steps to imagine yourself having it fully. Energies are moving and flowing all around us and even within us. Whether we like it or not, we are influenced by these energies, which manifest in spiritual, emotional, mental, and physical ways. When you engage in spellwork, you are making the decision to no longer passively allow yourself to be swept up in the energy currents around you. A spell summons up the natural power within you and releases it into the world with purpose.

The purpose is key to spellwork. Every single spell you cast begins with an intention. It can be as vague as being safe or as specific as "I want to make it home from work tonight without being attacked." Most spells are designed around a vague intention, with opportunities for you to customize the ritual work to appeal to more specific aspects of your life. Spells are designed this way for a reason. If your desired outcome is too specific, you'll need to summon a great deal of energy in order to make it happen. Broad, energetic goals are much easier to realize, with specific steps built into your spell to push that energy in a particular direction.

The word spell has some negative cultural connotations. You might be thinking of Halloween witches, bubbling cauldrons, or evil sorcerers from childhood or Hollywood movies. But a spell is just a powerful set of intentions, with ritualistic steps to put that intention out into the spiritual fabric of the world. By this definition, prayer is a kind of spell. Even daydreaming can be seen as spellwork, especially daydreams that sink deep into our subconscious and shape the way we communicate with the world.

If you are new to spellwork, it's important to remember that, when you cast a spell, you are contributing to the flow of energy that is already swirling around you. Sometimes our spells don't take simply because our spell is pushing against the energetic current. Sometimes that's a problem, and that's okay. We just have to adjust our ritual, cleanse our space, and maybe even re-word our intention. Sometimes that's just as it should be, and we are pushing for something that isn't actually right for us after all. As you begin casting spells, know that there is no right way or wrong way. Also, remember that everything you do has an energetic effect, whether you feel that effect or not. The intention is everything. If you are casting your spells with negative or faulty intentions, then that is the kind of energy you will manifest around you.

How Do Spells Work?

Energy, energy, energy. Spells are all about power, the natural power that wells up within us, and connects us to all things in the universe. Whether you know it or not, you are sending energy out into the world all the time and are also under the influence of energies coming at you from other beings. When you cast a spell, you are choosing to participate in that exchange of energy actively. This is what makes a spell different from meditation or even from simply setting a goal. Intention gives you direction, and the ceremonial components of the spell are what summon up the power you have within yourself to influence the world around you.

Every part of a spell is constructed in a way that will maximize your focus on your intention. To raise your energy to a level that is high enough to manifest whatever it is, you want your spell to accomplish. Whether you are speaking or writing words, performing actions, or visualizing certain things, every instruction in a spell is meant to maximize your focus. To direct your energy as much as possible in the direction you want it to go. If you are new to spellwork, it's best to follow the instructions as carefully as you can. Trust in the wisdom of your fellow practitioners and learn how spells are built. Notice how the ritualistic actions and words are designed to focus your attention. How they change your perspective on your life's situations even after you've ended your spell. As you become more experienced, you can begin to change or edit spells that you find in books or on the internet. You can even start writing your own spells! If you are a more seasoned practitioner, feel free to alter or edit the spells you find in this book as it makes sense for you.

Because spells are all about energy, they are often most potent at certain times of the year or during certain astrological events. There are several different astrological considerations that you can make when casting a spell. This includes the time of year, phase of the moon, and astrological positioning of the moon or other planets. The most powerful celestial body to consider when casting spells is the moon, with the sun coming in as a close second. Witches' calendar or datebook will tell you what astrological sign the moon is currently in, and a moon phase calendar will project the phases of the moon for the entire year. I would highly suggest getting yourself one or both of these resources, as appropriately timing your spells with the moon will significantly increase their potency.

3
WHEN DO YOU NEED PROTECTION?

There are many ways in which we are vulnerable to psychic attacks. Some attacks come at us from the spirit world, and some come directly from other magickal practitioners. But most often, we are exposed to negative psychic energies through everyday interactions, including digital ones.

Daily exposure to harmful psychic energy can be just as potent as an outright attack, and it can have the same effect. Psychic attacks can manifest themselves spiritually, but they can also make you feel emotionally unstable, mentally drained, or even physically unwell.

So the short answer to the question "When do you need protection?" is "All the time." This, however, isn't to sound paranoid or to intimate that negative energies surround you. In fact, most of the energies we are exposed to when working with the earth, other living beings, and even other people are positive. But all it takes is one bad interaction to forge a psychic tie between our own spirit and the negative energies of a specific person or place.

It's an unfortunate truth that, as we grow into power and confidence, the people around us will be more keen to test our boundaries. The more accomplished, successful, or fulfilled you are, the more vulnerable you are to the spiteful wishes of others. On the same note, people who are feeling threatened or insecure will often seek to undermine the safety and security of the people around them. Protection magick gives you the ability to safely navigate encounters with all kinds of people without putting your own emotional stability at risk.

Protection magick doesn't just protect us from external forces. Sometimes you may need a protection spell or charm to protect you from yourself. We are all vulnerable to inner voices of fear, anxiety, insecurity, and emotional trauma. This is a very normal and natural part of our human nature. But if we are overwhelmed by these inner voices, then our emotional and sometimes physical well-being is threatened. Protection magick gives us the ability to set boundaries in every realm and on every plane, both inner and outer.

On that note, we are sometimes at our most vulnerable to psychic attacks when we are feeling down about ourselves. When we are feeling anxious, depressed, or insecure, we can sometimes, literally, give away our power to others.

These are individuals whom we perceive to be stronger or wiser than we are. Those who love and care for us take this power and feed it back to us. They support us and help us to grow beyond the negative feelings that are bringing us low. Those who don't, however, can sometimes take advantage of this unbalanced exchange of power.

They begin to feed off our vulnerabilities, encouraging us to depend more and more on them until we are no longer able to fend for ourselves. Protection magick can help us to break free from these toxic relationships and take an energetic step back from people or situations that are not serving us.

Many protection spells will ask you to visualize images like walls, shields, or doorways. These visualizations are physical representations of emotional boundaries. Setting emotional boundaries can be incredibly tricky and defending those boundaries even more so. Even those who love us can often become angry or emotionally withholding when we stand up for what is truly important to us. This danger of conflict or rejection can cause us to feel guilty about caring for ourselves, and this feeling of guilt is what causes our boundaries to collapse. Protection magick, however, can help us to strengthen our emotional barriers. Give us the energy boost we need to defend ourselves against unhealthy feelings of responsibility or obligation to others.

Protection magick is actually best set when we are feeling healthy and stable. In times of crisis, it's too late to protect ourselves — we're already under attack. In these kinds of situations, cleansing or banishing spells are often more appropriate than defensive spellwork. Ironically, the best time to do protection work is when you're feeling safe. Protection is prevention, and protection magick often requires you to evaluate what is most important to you. Think about a very expensive safe, or a highly guarded bank vault. You would only store something in such a place that had extremely high value to you. Protection spells require a similar mentality. We simply don't have the strength to protect every single thing all the time. So when we cast a protection spell, we often have to focus our energies on the things that are most precious to us. When we are in a crisis, however, we are much less able to evaluate what those precious things really are critical. This is when we are less able to cast effective protective spells.

You definitely need protection when entering a place or engaging with people who are entirely new to you. Again, this is not to be paranoid or to live your life in fear of a psychic attack. But you never know what kinds of energies you're going to encounter when you are meeting someone for the first time, whether it's online or in person.

The same is true for moving into a new place or starting a new job. If you're going to be spending a lot of personal time in one place, then whatever psychic residue is clinging to that space will start to adhere to you too. When entering the unknown, it's definitely better to be safe than sorry, so times of change are definitely times to be working with protective magick.

Astrologically speaking, we are more vulnerable to psychic attacks during waxing and full moons than we are during the waning and full moons. Energy work done during a waxing or full moon is extremely powerful in drawing energetic influences toward us from the outside world. Therefore, when we open ourselves up to energetic forces, we can accidentally harness the power of the waxing or full moon to pull energies toward us if we aren't careful.

This tendency means that a waxing crescent, just after the new moon, is the best time to cast protective spells. Now, you can enter the more magnetic half of the monthly lunar cycle in safety.

Solar cycles work more subtly, but they follow a similar pattern. We are much more vulnerable to psychic attacks in the spring and summer than we are in the fall and winter because we are more energetically magnetic and open in the spring and summer months. Therefore, the best time to cast protective spells is really late winter or early spring. This is the time to prepare ourselves to safely emerge from the more meditative winter months into the warmer half of the year.

Your spirit is by far the most precious thing you have, so it is worth guarding. Working protective spells doesn't mean completely closing yourself off from others. It just means taking precautionary steps to make sure that unseen forces, intentional or accidental, aren't able to cause you harm. Psychic attacks are powerful and malicious, but the people and places we are exposed to on an everyday basis have the potential to cause us spiritual harm as well. So when do you need protection? All the time.

4

CASTING A CIRCLE

In Wicca and other magickal traditions, it's essential to cast a circle before engaging in any spellwork. When you are doing spellwork, you are opening yourself up to the flow of energy around you. This is necessary for your spell to take, but it can also make you vulnerable to negative or contradictory flows of energy that can disrupt or distort your spellwork. Casting a circle is essentially throwing up an energetic shield around your ritual space. This shield allows positive currents of energy to flow through your ritual space. It carries the intention of your spell out into the universe while simultaneously blocking negative or chaotic energies. Those energies may disrupt your working or, worse, cling to your ritual space after your spell has been cast.

The ritual drawing of protective circles doesn't originate with Wicca — it's something that has been an integral part of European magick for thousands of years.

Roman ambassadors would draw circles around themselves with the end of a staff to indicate that they should be protected from harm. Babylonians would draw a circle of flour around the bed of a sick person to protect them from demons and other malignant spirits. German Jews in the medieval period would draw a circle around the bed of a woman in labor for the same reason (Buckland, 1986).

In today's spiritual traditions, there are different methods of circle casting, with slightly different visualizations, chants, and movements. Some ways require words to be spoken; some don't. Some people are content to draw the circle with their finger or hand, while others prefer to draw the circle with an altar tool, whether that be a wand, athame, sword, staff, feather, incense, or smudging bundle. You can physically mark the circle on the floor with a length of the chord, draw it directly on the floor or carpet with a piece of chalk, or even paint the circle on the floor. If you are restricted by logistical concerns, like sharing space, or simply prefer to visualize, that's okay too. At the end of the day, it's the ritual drawing of the circle and the accompanying visualization that gives the circle its power, so an imaginary circle is just as potent as a physical one.

At the end of this chapter, you will find a basic circle-casting and releasing technique that you are free to change, adapt, or edit as you wish. That being said, when casting (sometimes called "opening") the circle, you should begin in the east and always draw the circle in a clockwise direction. It is also important to remember that if you choose to work within a circle, it should be cast before you begin any spellwork. Most spells won't really list circle casting as a step, but if you're working with circles, assuming that casting the circle is the first step in your spell.

The same is true in the end. The circle is not only cast to protect you from external influences. It also helps to keep in the power you're raising up during the process of your spell.

After your ritual is done, in order to release into the universe these energies that you've raised, you need to release, or close, the circle that you cast. Again, most spells won't outline casting and releasing circles in the list of steps, so assume that, if you cast a circle at the beginning, your last step should be to release the circle.

As with the circle-casting technique given in this chapter, you are free to edit the circle-releasing ritual as you wish, with one exception. Like casting the circle, when releasing, you should begin at the circle's easternmost point. However, when discharging, you should always move in a counterclockwise direction.

At no point during a magickal working should you leave the circle once it's been cast. However, if there is an emergency or exceptional circumstance, you can cut a doorway to leave and re-enter the circle safely. The proper procedure for leaving and re-entering the circle will be given at the end of this chapter.

Basic Circle Casting

1. Sit or kneel in front of your altar with your eyes closed.
2. Imagine yourself enclosed in a ball of white light.
3. Imagine the ball of light expanding out to enclose you in a sphere about five feet in diameter.
4. Maintain this image in your mind for a moment. Next, consciously relax all of the muscles in your body.
5. Open your eyes, stand, and move to stand just inside the eastern point of the circle.
6. Point the forefinger of your dominant hand down at the circle line.
7. Walk slowly around the inside of the circle, "drawing" the line of the circle with your finger.

8. Once you have completed the circle, return to your altar, which should now be sitting in the center of the drawn circle.
9. Light the candles and/or incense on the altar.
10. Hold your hands over a small bowl of salt pre-prepared on the altar.
11. Say these words: *"Let this salt be pure and let it purify my life, as I used it in this rite, dedicated to _____* [insert the name(s) of whichever deities or spirits you are invoking during your spell here], *in whom I believe."*
12. Take three pinches of salt and drop them into a small bowl of water.
13. Mix the water in the bowl in a clockwise direction with your finger.
14. Say these words: *"Let the sacred salt drive out any impurities in this water that together they may be used in the service of these rites and at any time and in any way I may use them."*
15. Take the bowl of salted water to the easternmost point of the circle. Sprinkle the water around the edges of the circle in a clockwise direction.
16. Return to the altar and light four candles.
17. Place them at the four direction points of the circle, beginning with the east, and then moving to the south, then the west, and last the north.
18. Return to the altar and say these words: *"The sacred circle has been cast. I am here in peace and love of my own free will."*
19. Begin the first step of your spell.

Basic Circle Releasing

1. Complete the last step of your spell.

2. Extinguish the candle at the northern point of the circle, then move to the west, the south, and the east.
3. Once the candles have been properly stored away, return to the easternmost point of the circle.
4. Point to the circle line with the forefinger of your dominant hand.
5. Walk counterclockwise around the inside edge of the circle, tracing the line of the circle with your finger.
6. Once you have completed the circle, return to the altar and say these words: *"The sacred circle has been released. Let the work that has been done here be sent forth into the universe to do as I have wished."*

Leaving the Circle

With your finger or an altar tool, stand at the easternmost point of the circle. Make a slashing motion across the line of the circle, first on the right, then on the left. This will cut two lines in the circle to form a doorway through which you may now leave.

Re-entering the Circle

Once you have re-entered the circle through the same door you cut when you left, close the doorway by drawing the line of the circle in a clockwise direction with your finger or with an altar tool. If you consecrated the circle with water or incense at the beginning, then you should consecrate the re-drawn line again.

5
WORKING WITHOUT A CIRCLE

Though familiar to Wiccan magick and recommended for beginning practitioners, not all pagan or magickal practitioners cast circles. This is for a variety of reasons. Some individuals and/or covens adhere to magickal traditions that didn't historically use circles. Others engage in different practices that achieve the same goals — protecting the sacred ritual space and harnessing the sacred energies before releasing them out into the universe.

If casting circles is something that isn't in your practice, you're in good company. However, if you decide that casting circles aren't for you, then you need to have excellent protection and cleansing habits in your ritual space. Spellwork makes you incredibly vulnerable to psychic energy, so you need to ensure that you are protected when you enter the ritual space.

Perhaps the most common alternative to casting a circle is to set up protective wards around a ritual space. For example, before a Catholic church is built, the foundations are ritually blessed to consecrate the ground as sacred space. This is done to ensure, while they are inside, all who enter the church are protected from evil influences. In neo-pagan and magickal traditions, many people choose to do something similar, especially if they have one dedicated room or corner for ritual work. Protective guardians can be activated and set up at the four directional corners of a room. A particular indoor or outdoor space can be cleansed and consecrated as a sacred ritual space.

However you choose to protect your ritual space, if you're not casting circles, then it's also vital to regularly re-activate your protective wards. It's also important to periodically cleanse your ritual space. If you aren't working with circles, then I would recommend cleansing after every spell you cast, to ensure that your area is energetically clean when you return to cast a new spell.

Some practitioners, especially those who are solitary or who move around a lot, choose to protect their own bodies and auras rather than casting protective wards around a particular ritual space. Choosing this path essentially means ensuring that your personal aura is protected from harmful influences when you engage in ritual work; therefore, you can safely practice no matter where you are. In a way, this method is more straightforward than casting circles or consecrating ritual spaces, but it requires much higher maintenance. When you cast a circle, you can be sure that you are safe within the confines of that circle. The same is true if you enter a protective ritual enclave. But if you are protecting your own aura, you need to be absolutely sure to activate your protection every single time you cast a spell. You also need to make sure that you cleanse yourself after every ritual. It is one thing to have residual magickal energies clinging to your ritual space, but it's another to have those energies clinging to your spiritual person.

There are several different techniques to protect both a ritual space and your spiritual person. This chapter will give two methods — one that will protect your ritual space and one that will protect your spiritual person. Both of these techniques are powerful alternatives to casting a circle that will both protect your space and harness the energies of your spells.

A Witch's Bottle: Protecting the Spiritual Person

1. Find and clean a bottle or jar. Any kind will do. You can choose a Mason jar, coffee container, or even an empty beer bottle as long as you thoroughly wash and clean it.
2. Fill the bottle or jar halfway with sharp objects, such as broken glass, old razor blades, rusty nails and screws, pins, needles, etc.
3. When the jar is half-full with these objects, urinate into the bottle to fill it up. If you are someone who menstruates, getting a little bit of menstrual blood into the bottle can be quite powerful, as well.
4. Cover and seal the jar. This is a significant step for health and safety reasons. Coating the jar or bottle's original cover with a few extra layers of duct tape is recommended.
5. Now bury the jar in the ground, at least twelve inches deep. The jar can be buried or hidden in any location, but you should take care to choose a place where it won't be disturbed. As long as the bottle remains safely buried underground, you are protected from evil influences, no matter where you go or how far from the bottle you are. This spell is strong enough to protect you in place of a circle because it doesn't just shield you from evil influences; it acts as a kind of

psychic mirror, reflecting negative energies at their point of origin.
6. This spell should last indefinitely, but if you can't be sure that your bottle has remained undisturbed, it's recommended to renew this spell once a year.

Wards: Protecting the Ritual Space

When erecting wards, you have a few different options. You can ask specific deities, spirits, or even ancestors to guard your ritual space from danger. With animal spirits, you can do the same. You can use protective runes, words, or other symbols. You can work with the elements, using candles for fire, running water, incense burners for air, or stones for the Earth. No matter what you choose, the important thing is to set one up in each of the four compass points around your altar. For example, if you prefer to work with the water element, you can set up a small fountain in the east, south, west, and north. It's tough for negative energy to pass through running water.

You can do the same with four candles or four mini altars to different deities, ancestors, or animal spirits. If you choose to use elemental objects or protective symbols, you should regularly cleanse your guardians after each spell to ensure that they remain strong and active. If you are working with guardian spirits, you should periodically leave offerings on their mini altars to thank them for their protection and to ensure that they have the energy to continue defending you.

The first time you designate your wards, follow the steps outlined in chapter 4 to cast a circle. Replace the four directional candles with your four guardians; however, you choose to represent them. Once your guardians are activated, there is no need to "close" the protective circle. Leave your guardians erected around your ritual space — if you take them down or put them away, you are stripping them of their power, and you'll have to consecrate them all over again when you next set them up.

After you've consecrated your guardians, there's no need to consecrate them again. Unless you take them down, that is. Instead of casting a circle every time you do a spell, simply activate your guardians before engaging in ritual work. For example, if you're using candles or incense, light them before you engage in your spellwork. You can activate spirits by anointing their statues with oil or changing out their offerings. Make sure to enable your guardians in a clockwise direction, starting from the easternmost point. When you deactivate them, make sure to do so in a counterclockwise direction, starting from the easternmost point. These guardians will essentially do the energetic work that you do with your own power when you cast a circle.

6

YOUR ALTAR

You can utilize just about anything you want for an altar. If your ritual space is outside, you can use a flat rock or a tree stump. If your ritual space is inside, you can use a small coffee table, a wooden box, or a corner of your desk. You can even lay a few loose wooden boards over a stack of bricks. As long as it's flat and in a place where it won't be disturbed, you can be as imaginative as you wish when setting up your altar.

The only "rule" to consider when choosing an altar space is metal. Iron and steel, in particular, are highly conductive metals. This means that power travels quickly and easily through them. This is true of physical power like electricity, but it's also true of magickal power. Therefore, it's typically recommended that your altar not contain any iron or steel, as this can make it much more difficult to control the flow of magick in and out of your space. This is especially true if you are working without a circle.

Your altar can be any shape or size, but the ideal shape for magickal work is a circle. This is why rocks and tree stumps make such good altars out in the natural world. Believe it or not, circles are sacred shapes in almost every culture because they allow for a smooth and gentle flow of energy. However, a circular altar is far from necessary. If you find yourself restricted in terms of space or finances, don't worry! There is no "wrong" size or shape for an altar space.

Just as you can choose anything you want for an altar, you can also furnish your altar however you choose. Some magickal traditions have specific "guidelines" for altar furniture, but these are usually just that — guidelines. If you're new to the practice and aren't sure where to start, Wicca, too, has some altar guidelines to get you started.

The basic altar setup for a Wiccan altar typically consists of the following:

- At least one candle
- An incense burner also known as a censer
- A small bowl of salt and a small bowl of water
- A libation or offering plate
- At least one goblet
- Statues to represent deities and/or spirits

If you are someone who tends to perform ritual work at night or in the dark, then you definitely want to have multiple candles on your altar, as electric light is not recommended for a ritual space.

If you already have an altar, however, there are a few rituals you can do to optimize your altar space for protective purposes. Below are a few items you can ritually add to your altar space that will act as (semi) permanent fixtures on your altar to keep negative energies away from you and your ritual space.

Choosing a Tarot Guardian

The cards of the tarot aren't arbitrary — each card of the tarot deck has symbolic magickal power. As such, you can dedicate a card of the tarot to protect you or your altar space.

To set a tarot guardian, choose a card from a tarot or oracle deck that you feel a strong, energetic connection to. Place the card in the middle of your altar. Preferably on top of a pentacle or other representation of the Earth element. For the next thirty days, visualize the scene of the card every morning or just before you go to bed. Imagine that the borders of the card are actually a doorway. The scene on the card is simply a glimpse into a parallel world. Visualize the beings, spirits, or elements of the card coming through this doorway and into your ritual space. Each day that you do this, you will feel a stronger and stronger connection to the energies of the card, and you will automatically begin to feel those connections each time you step into your ritual space. After thirty days, you may return the card to your deck (if you wish), secure in the knowledge that you are now infused with and protected by the energies of this card. Renew this ritual once a year.

Flower Petal Altar Renewal

You can buy flowers from a local shop for this cleansing ritual, but flowers picked from your yard, or a local park will be much more potent. While picking flowers, notice the color of the petals. These colors represent the areas of your practice that need to be healed and renewed. Yellow petals represent creativity, red is for passion, blue is for emotion, green is for stability, orange is for health, and white is for cleanliness.

Once you have picked your flowers, pluck off the petals and scatter them gently over your altar space. Imagine them as symbolic of a cleansing rain, wiping away all negativity from your altar space. Imagine them revitalizing and renewing the various color-specific energies, and imagine those energies washing over your altar surface, tools, and statues. After sprinkling these petals across your altar, leave them there for about a month or until they have completely dried out. Then gather the dried petals and store them for future magickal workings.

Mighty Dead Candle

Most magickal practitioners choose to build close spiritual relationships with deities and spirits. However, ancestor worship is a pillar of many spiritual traditions around the world, especially in Asia. Ancestors can be particularly powerful guardians because they are connected to you by familial and/or cultural legacy.

For this candle, choose from among the dead someone that you would like to honor on your altar as a protective entity. This person can be someone who is related to you or someone that you admire.

Once you've chosen your spirit, carve their name into a dedicated candle. Place a picture of that person on your altar, and place the candle on top of the picture. If there are no photographs or official portraits of the person you've chosen, a speculative portrait or more abstract representation is okay too. For example, I have no pictures of my grandfather, but I do have a small box that he kept for tools. When doing this ritual, I would place my candle on top of his toolbox since I have no pictures to use.

Once the candle is secured in a holder on top of your picture or representation, say these words:

Let the flame of this candle guide you

to the warmth and love of my sacred space.

Your Altar

Let this invitation be

a welcome light that you embrace.

Watch over my rites with

benevolence and mystery,

and forever

the protector of my altar, you will be!

Light the candle when you are doing ritual work to invite the mighty dead to watch over your working.

Creating an Ancestor Altar

You can take the concept of the mighty dead candle one step further and create an entirely separate altar to honor your ancestors.

An ancestor altar is really a traditional fixture in Japanese and Korean homes and is a standard spiritual fixture of many traditions around the world.

An ancestor altar doesn't have to be in the same place as your ritual altar, as the ancestors you honor on the altar will be protecting you wherever you go. An ancestor altar should typically be covered with an altar cloth and covered with items or pictures that remind you of those who have passed. Representations of the four elements (air, fire, water, and earth) should be placed at the four compass points of the ancestor altar. Candles are traditionally used for light, but a small string of LED lights can make the altar space a bit more cheerful and can be left on whenever you are home.

Once you have initially set up the altar, boil two tablespoons of dried lavender in a small pot. When the water is steaming, place the pot on a towel or rubber pad on the altar and say these words:

Be always with me.

Watch over me and never truly

be gone. That which lives in spirit never dies.

To give your ancestors the respect and power they need to be your spiritual guardians, leave offerings of food, and drink on the altar. Change out the offerings on your ancestors' birthdays or other significant dates.

7

OBJECTS OF PROTECTION

There are certain objects you can wear to protect your physical and spiritual person and to keep you safe from harm no matter wherever you go.

Amulets

Amulets are items in Nature that, in and of themselves, are imbued with protective energies. An amulet, therefore, isn't something that you make. It's something that you find. A bear's claw, a rabbit's foot, and a four-leaf clover are all amulets. Sometimes associated with "good luck," these three magickal items are naturally suffused with protective energies. Wearing these items as jewelry or placing them on your altar will go a long way toward keeping you safe from negative energies. A very powerful amulet is a stone with a hole through it.

Amulets are often most worn as necklaces, but you can also carry them in your pocket, or fashion them into other kinds of jewelry. Necklaces are the preferred way to wear amulets because they are easy to hide. You can easily tuck your amulet under your clothing, and no one will be any the wiser. You can also place amulets on your altar to protect yourself and your ritual space. You can even give amulets as gifts of protection to the people that you care about.

Amulets can also be useful for protecting spaces that aren't your altar space. For example, it's tricky to do a cleansing ritual of your workspace. But a small amulet on your desk or in your locker will often go unnoticed by coworkers and can be quite powerful as a protective tool. The same is true for your technology. Placing a small amulet next to your computer or attaching it to your phone or keys as a charm can bring you protection in your daily interactions. Keeping an amulet in your wallet or purse can have a similar effect. Many people choose to hang amulets from the rearview mirrors of their cars for protection on the road. You can also store amulets in your glove compartment. Or still, in the trunk of your vehicle for the same purpose.

Anything important to you can be protected with an amulet. If you are a musician, you can store an amulet in the case of your instrument. If you are a software developer, you can put an amulet in the pocket of your laptop bag. If you need protection from a specific person, you can place an amulet on your altar over a picture (or other representation) of the person who is giving you grief. To protect your home, you can hang amulets in the windows, attach them to the railings of a balcony, or hang them from the eaves of a porch.

Charm Bags

Charm bags are small bags that are filled with a mix of items that, together, have protective energies that keep the wearer or the space safe from harm. You can attach a charm bag to a string and wear it as a necklace, or you can keep it in your pocket to protect yourself wherever you go. Below are two charm bags (sometimes called "sachets") that you can make to protect yourself from specific troubles.

Fire Web Charm Bag (Ravenwolf, 2019)

This is a charm bag for general protection, using the element of fire and a deity or spirit of your choice. To make it, you will need the following:

- A paper or cloth image of a deity of your choice
- A purple ribbon
- Dragon's blood resin
- Nettles
- Ginger
- Cinnamon
- Galangal
- Cloves
- Brick dust

Put the herbs in the middle of the paper or cloth. Set an intention by asking the deity you've chosen to protect you. You can ask for a specific kind of protection.

For example:

I ask that _____ protect me from conflict during the coming holiday.

Or you can ask for more general protection:

I ask that _____ keep me safe from harm and shielded from negativity.

Whisper your request directly over the paper or cloth, so close that the herbs should be slightly disturbed with the wind of your breath. Once you've made your request, roll the cloth or paper away from you. Then gather up the edges and tie them tightly with the purple ribbon to form a small bag. Hang the bag near your front door or in a window.

Charm Bag for Financial Security

This charm bag will protect you from financial troubles. To make it, you will need the following:

- A piece of green cloth
- A green marker
- Coins
- Pine needles
- Cinnamon or cloves
- A green ribbon

First, draw the symbol of whatever currency you use most ($ for Americans) on the green cloth with the green marker. Beneath the currency symbol, write your name. Place the coins, pine needles, and herbs in the center of the cloth, then fold up the edges and tie them tightly with the ribbon to form a small bag. As you do this, say these words:

My wealth is secure, so mote it be.

Hang the bag somewhere near your front door or leave it next to your computer if you manage most of your finances online.

Talismans

A talisman is a man-made object that serves the same purpose as an amulet. While amulets are natural objects, talismans are specifically crafted to bring the wearer protection from negative energies. Talismans can be purchased, or they can be made. For example, a crucifix can be considered a talisman for a Catholic or Christian wearer. However, the most powerful talismans are the ones that are made by you personally.

Talismans can come in any shape or size. There are only two essential steps when it comes to the making of a talisman. The first one is the inscription. Most talismans are labeled or carved with protective symbols. The second is consecration, or infusing the talisman with the magickal energy it needs to serve as an energetic shield.

Talismans can be made of any material, including paper, silver, copper, lead, stone, etc. But traditionally, talismans are made of metal. Different metals correspond to different energies; therefore, it's best to choose a metal that is most closely associated with the energies you want to invoke and/or protect yourself from. Below is a table of metal correspondences to help you choose the best metals for your own talismans:

- **Gold** — fortune, hope, money
- **Silver** — merchandise, dreams, theft
- **Mercury** — debt, fear, loss
- **Tin** — honor, riches, clothing, desires
- **Copper** — love, friendship, strangers
- **Lead** — life, building, doctrine, protection (general)

Mercury, however, is both a liquid metal and a highly poisonous one. If you want to use mercury to make a talisman, be extremely careful when handling it. Talismans that use mercury often contain it in a small bottle or a glass container. However, an easier and safer alternative to mercury is parchment. Believe it or not, parchment paper has similar magickal energies and can be used to make potent talismans with the same correspondences as mercury.

Hand-made talismans don't have to be carved from raw materials. Coins, for example, can be very easily converted into talismans and are made from a variety of different metals.

Once you've chosen your metal, it's time to choose an inscription. The most powerful way to make talismans is to write, carve, or trace symbols of personalization on one side and symbols of objective on the other side.

Symbols of personalization can include your name, birthdate, personal magickal symbol. It can consist of the astrological symbol of your sun, rising, or moon sign, or even the astrological symbol of your sun sign's ruling planet. Essentially, the symbol of personalization is any symbol that can be associated with you and/or your personality. These words or symbols can be written in any alphabet and with any tools. They can be carved, painted, or traced with oil.

Symbols of your objective are symbols that have to do with the intention of your talisman. For a protective talisman, you'll want to choose a word or symbol that you associate with protection, safety, or shielding.

If all of this seems a bit too open-ended, not to worry. There are plenty of instructions and spells for how to make protective talismans that will tell you which metals and symbols are best to use. But don't be afraid to experiment — the more personal your talisman, the more potent it will be.

8

PERSONAL PROTECTION

This chapter will provide instructions for several spells you can cast to protect yourself, your spaces, and your loved ones from harm.

Wipe Away Negativity (Kambos, 2019)

This spell is most potent during the winter season, especially during the month of January.

January 4 is the feast of Epiphany, traditionally celebrated by Christians as the day the Three Wise Men met the baby Jesus. Today, some Christians in Central Europe will chalk the initials of the Wise Men on their front doors during this feast to protect their homes from evil spirits. Inspired by this tradition, this spell for personal protection can also be used to banish a bad habit in the early months of the year. For this spell, you will need the following:

- A small flat stone
- White chalk
- An eraser

- Bottled spring water
- A clean cloth

First, bless the stone by wiping it clean with the spring water and cloth. You may say a blessing if you wish. Next write whatever it is you want to banish or protect yourself from on the surface of the stone with the chalk. Think for a few moments about this problem. Then vigorously erase the chalk from the stone with the eraser or the cloth. As you do this, visualize your problem as being wiped away. Once the chalk has been erased, clean the stone one more time with the water, and place it on your altar.

Solar Stone as a Winter Light (Digitalis, 2019)

This spell is most potent during the month of January, especially during a waning moon.

Whether or not you live in a place that experiences snowfall, the winter months are typically the darkest months of the year. This spell will help you to reconnect with the warmth of the sun and bring a little solar energy into the winter darkness. For this spell, you will need the following:

- A shoe
- A sock
- An orange stone (either a crystal or a stone you've painted orange)
- Cinnamon

During the daylight hours, hold the orange stone up to the sun and imagine it being filled to the brim with solar energy. Say these words:

This stone is alchemized,

magnetized, and charged by the conquering sun.

Put the stone into the sock and sprinkle in a little cinnamon. Then roll up the sock with the stone and tuck it into the shoe. Place the shoe with the sock inside on your altar and leave it there until the spring equinox.

Woven Protection for the Notorious (Pesznecker, 2019)

This spell is most potent during the spring season, especially during the month of March.

This is a spell for the protection of a loved one, whether near or far. For this spell, you will need the following:

- Six pieces of paper
- A black pen
- A blue pen
- A small bowl of salted water
- One lit candle
- Glue

On both sides of the first piece of paper, write the name of the person you wish to protect with the black pen. On the second piece, write "**WATER**" on both sides. On the third piece, write "**EARTH**" on both sides. Sprinkle a bit of the saltwater over all three papers and leave to dry. On the fourth piece of paper, write "**AIR**" on both sides. On the fifth piece, write "**FIRE**" on both sides. Pass all five papers safely through the smoke above the burning candle. On the sixth piece of paper, write the name of the person you wish to protect on both sides, but this time, use the blue pen. This should be the only paper that uses the blue pen.

Once you are finished, roll up each piece of paper and wrap them tightly around each other, adding small dots of glue to hold them in place. Once you have finished, set the wrapped papers on your altar and say these words:

Earth, air, fire, water,

by the power of these elements, you are protected and blessed!

Protection Ring and Spell Jar (Furie, 2019)

This spell is most potent during the month of March, especially during a waxing moon.

This is a powerful protection spell that will protect both you and your ritual space. For this spell, you will need the following:

- One tablespoon nettle
- One tablespoon mint
- One tablespoon mullein
- One tablespoon oregano
- One small Mason jar
- Soy or vegetable oil
- A ring that will fit comfortably on your middle finger

Combine all of these herbs and put them into the jar. Then pour in enough oil to fill the jar to the top. Empower the jar by placing your hands over the open mouth, visualizing protective energy coursing from your hands down into the jar. Then take the ring, dip it into the oil, and place it on the middle finger of your dominant hand. Once you've consecrated the ring, seal the jar tightly and set it on your altar. On the full moon, shake the jar like a snow globe to give the magick some extra power.

Passover Meal (Whitehurst, 2019)

This spell is most potent in the spring season, especially during the month of April.

Passover is the Jewish holiday that commemorates the liberation of the Hebrews from slavery in Egypt. Whether or not you are Jewish, this holiday brings with it extremely powerful magickal energy and is a great time to do some protective rituals. Take some time to learn about the Seder meal. A traditional meal had at night during the week of Passover. Plan this Seder meal to respect or honor the struggles and liberations from your own past, whether these are personal liberations, or the liberations of historical groups to which you belong (for example, your family, your ethnic group, spiritual or religious community, the LGBTQ+ community, etc.). Traditional fixtures of the Seder meal include matzo ball soup, four glasses of wine, and the absence of leavened bread. However, as you learn about the Seder traditions, feel free to adapt the rituals to make sense of the struggles and/or people that you are choosing to honor as well as for the efforts that you or your group are still battling.

Eggscellent Spell (Zakroff, 2019)

This spell is most potent in the month of April, especially during a waning moon.

Whether or not you celebrate the Easter holiday, several spiritual traditions like to dye eggs at this time of year. If you are part of a tradition that colors eggs, save the colored shells, and use them in this protection spell.

Grind the colored shells with a mortar and pestle. Bring the ground shells outside and move around your home (or apartment building) in a clockwise direction, lightly scattering the powdered shells on the ground. This shell circle will energetically protect you from harm and will add nutrients to the soil.

End a Curse Spell

This spell is most potent during a waning moon, especially when the moon is in Capricorn.

Just as the rains wash the earth, this spell will help you to wash away or remove any negativity from your life, especially if you are the victim of a curse or psychic attack. For this spell, you will need the following:

- A lemon
- A knife
- Ground black pepper

Think about the person or situation that is causing you problems. Slash open the skin of the lemon in several places. Sprinkle the black pepper over the lemon and rub it into the slashes. Take the lemon out to a secluded place and smash or stomp on it. While you do this, say these words:

By pepper, rain, and lemon cleansed,

This problem now ends.

Simply walk away. The spell is done, and the curse is broken.

9
PROTECTION FOR YOUR HOME

Much of what happens in our lives that have emotional and spiritual importance occurs in the home. This makes our homes one of the most sacred spaces in our lives, but it can also make our homes vulnerable to psychic attacks. This chapter outlines several protective spells you can cast to keep your home shielded and safe.

12Protection Charm for the Bedroom (Calafia, 2019)

This spell is most potent during a waning moon, especially when the moon is in Aquarius.

During the spring season, all parts of nature are most vulnerable to sexual energies, humans included. When positive, sexual energies are some of the most powerful, we can tap into. But when negative, they can be some of the most destructive forces we ever encounter. This spell will keep you safe during the spring (or any) season from rampaging sexual energies, either from within yourself or coming to you from an external source. For this spell, you will need the following:

- Rose
- Pine
- Cedar
- Nutmeg
- Ginger
- Lavender
- Lemon
- Yarrow
- Mugwort
- Sage
- Barley
- Echinacea
- A small crystal of your choice
- A cowrie shell
- A small bowl
- A small cloth of any color
- A ribbon or string of any color

First, blend all of the herbs together in the bowl. Visualize a bright, protective circle growing out from the center of the bowl until it encompasses the entire mix. Place the crystal and the cowrie shell in the center of the cloth. Pour the herbal mix over them. Pull up the four edges of the cloth and tie them tightly together with a ribbon to form a small pouch. Hang the bag in the doorway of your bedroom, or keep it under your pillow.

Earth Protection Spell (Freuler, 2019)

This spell is most potent during the spring season, especially during the month of May.

It's easy to forget that our homes are physical spaces intimately connected to the land. This is especially easy to forget if we live in an apartment or on a boat. This spell reconnects you to the land on which you live and asks the earth element itself to protect your space from harm. For this spell, you will need the following:

- A small piece of paper
- A pen
- A small bottle or jar with a lid
- A small handful of dirt

On the piece of paper, write down the "name" of your home. This can be your mailing address, apartment number, or even the name of your building. Put the paper into the bottle or jar, and sprinkle the dirt over the paper. Say these words:

Around this earth, I build a wall.

Within this earth, I have a space to hide.

Sharp as a claw, strong as a rock,

guarding what's inside.

Place the jar on your altar. Your home is now "hidden" from malicious or harmful energies.

Setting Tarot Guardians for Your Home (Ardinger, 2019)

This spell is most potent in the summer season, especially during the month of June.

Just as you can set a tarot guardian to protect yourself or your altar, you can ask tarot guardians to watch over your home. First, set the card for the Empress (major arcana III) and the Emperor (major arcana IV) on your altar side-by-side. Then set the card for the Fool (major arcana 0) and the Magician (major arcana I) underneath the Emperor and the Empress, side-by-side. The four cards should form a tight square in the center of your altar. In the center of the square, where the four corners of the cards touch, place a small stone from your yard or property.

Visualize the four figures on the cards standing guard at the four corners of your home. As long as you keep the cards on your altar, your home will be protected from harm.

Candle Banishment Spell (Mankey, 2019)

This spell is most potent in the month of June, especially during a waxing moon.

Psychic attacks aren't only targeted at people. Sometimes our homes can come under attack as well. Whether someone is jealous of what you have or wishes to break up the relationships of all who live under your roof, attacks on the home can be extremely harmful, as they affect all who live there. If your home is under a psychic attack and you know where the negative energies are coming from, this candle spell can help you to break the curse and defend your home. For this spell, you will need the following:

- One small candle of any color
- A sharp object or magickal tool

Carve the name of the person or group that is causing trouble for your home or living situation on the sides of the candle. As you carve the name, think banishing thoughts like "**Leave us alone,**" "**Go away,**" "**Bother other people,**" and "**With harm to none,**" (you want whoever is bothering you to leave you alone, but there's no reason to hurt them in-kind). Light the candle and visualize the hot wax burning that person or people's influence out of your home.

Cloaking Spell for the Home

This spell is most potent in the summer season, especially during the month of July.

Fight or flight are often the two choices we have as people when confronted with danger. But our homes have a third option — they can be hidden from negative influences. This spell will help your home to be "cloaked" or made invisible to malicious energies. For this spell, you will need the following:

- Amaranth
- Lemon peel
- Mugwort
- Mistletoe
- Olive oil

Mix together the herbs in a small bowl. Pour an ample amount of olive oil over the herbs, and mix well with your finger or a magickal tool. While you're mixing, say these words:

Hidden like the wind,

hidden like the depths of the sea so deep,

hidden like a spider's web, gossamer silent,

this home will not be seen!

Using your finger or a small paintbrush, rub a small amount of the oil and herb mixture onto both sides of the front door frame. Renew this spell once a year. It will keep your home invisible to those who wish harm to those who are inside.

Shielding Spell During Sun in Cancer

This spell is most potent during the month of July, especially during a waning moon.

During the month of July, the sun moves into the astrological sign of Cancer. The sign of Cancer rules home and family; therefore, this is a particularly powerful time to cast protective spells over our homes and those who live with us. For this spell, you will need the following:

- One small piece of black tourmaline for each person that lives with you in your home, plus one (for example, if five people are living in your home, including you, you will need six pieces of tourmaline)

Take one piece of tourmaline and hold it tightly in your fist. Say these words:

Tourmaline, lend your might.

Protect this home from everything but light.

Guard and defend,

and our energy mend!

Place this stone on the sill of an east- or south-facing window in the home. Now give the other pieces of tourmaline to each person in your house, and save one for yourself. Keep the stone in your pocket, and you will be protected by this spell even when you leave your home.

10
RECOGNIZING ATTACKS

The world is an energetically complex place. Sometimes adverse events, feelings, or experiences come into our path by chance. However, occasionally, negative experiences are willed at us. Someone actively wishes us harm, and their negative wishes are so powerful that they begin to manifest in our thoughts and our lives. This is a psychic attack (Fortune, 1930). Sometimes psychic attacks are calculated and come from another magickal practitioner. When this happens, we call it a curse or a hex. But more often than not, psychic attacks come from people who don't realize how powerful their energies are. They send negative or harmful energies at us without realizing that those energies can and do manifest in real life.

So how do you identify if you're under attack or if you're just caught in unfortunate circumstances? How do you know if the negativity in your life is coming from within (yes, we can psychically sabotage ourselves) or from an external force? And if you are under attack, how do you know where the attack is coming from?

The main difference between psychic attack and just plain old bad luck is energy. Of course, we never feel good when bad things happen to us. We may feel sad, angry, hopeless, or even sink into depression. But when we are caught in negative circumstances, we have resilience. No matter how horrible, sad, or unjust the event may be, we have inner reserves of strength that we tap into in the worst moments of our lives to help us to push through.

When we are under psychic attack, however, those reserves of power are being drained away. Psychic attacks make us feel powerless, despairing, and hopeless. We feel fuzzy-headed and incapable of handling even the slightest challenges. We either project our feelings of powerlessness out on to others, becoming irritable and reckless, or we internalize our feeling of helplessness and become despairing and guilt-ridden. Psychic attacks rarely manifest as tragedy or terrible events. Rather, psychic attacks leech away our ability to love and participate in the world. This lack of power and energy can create dire circumstances when we become distant from our loved ones or stop performing up to our potential at work (Fortune, 1930).

If you have ever experienced significant depression, bipolar, or other psychological symptoms of what are classified as "mood disorders," then the above symptoms might sound eerily familiar. Our brains are chemically quite complicated, and mental illness can be just as easily triggered by our past memories and inner feelings as they can be from external forces. Psychic attacks don't necessarily cause mental illness, but they can often trigger these illnesses and disrupt our ability to care for ourselves. Whether or not you have a diagnosis, remember that self-care is the number-one step to fighting off psychic attacks (Blackwood, 2019). Just as others have the raw power to make us feel drained and unwell, remember that you also have the natural ability to shield yourself from these attacks.

As magickal practitioners, however, we can take protective steps to shield ourselves from random or residual negative energies whenever we encounter strangers or enter new spaces. However, a focused psychic attack can sometimes be powerful enough to break through our basic defenses (Blackwood, 2019). It's at that point that more powerful banishing and cleansing rituals are necessary to free ourselves from the curse that's been placed over us. But the first step, of course, is recognizing that curse in the first place.

In almost all cases of assault or abuse, the perpetrator is someone who knows the victim. This, unfortunately, is also true of a psychic attack. In very rare cases, we can be caught in the negative energies of strangers or even entities from the spirit realm (Buckland, 1986). But if you have erected even the most basic of psychic defenses, it's far more likely that, if you are under psychic attack, it's from someone that you know and interact with daily.

If you believe you are under a psychic attack, it's crucial to observe your energy levels. If you are a more introverted individual, then prolonged levels of social contact are probably draining for you, no matter how healthy or enriching the relationship. But introverted or not, after spending time with loved ones, we should feel a healthy kind of tired. We should feel warm, loved, and spiritually enriched.

However, if you spend time with someone, and after even a small conversation, you feel exhausted, anxious, or irritable, this is a red flag. You aren't going to love or even like everyone that you meet. Still, if you leave a conversation with someone feeling utterly drained of energy, there's probably something more sinister going on than a simple personality conflict. If at all possible, minimize the contact that you have with this person, and that includes digital communication. Psychic connections are forged just as easily in cyberspace as they are in real life.

If this is someone that, at least for right now, you have to interact with on a daily basis, then take extreme caution. Protect yourself as much as you can. Make a talisman, amulet, or charm bag to keep you safe when you are around this person. Cast a curse-breaking spell and leave it on your altar until you are able to get this person out of your daily life. If things are really bad for you emotionally, you might need to move beyond protection magick and cast a cleansing ritual to rid yourself of their influence.

When we forge intense emotional connections with others, we also build spiritual relationships. This is how we can somehow "sense" when our loved ones are happy or sad, sick or healthy, even when they aren't physically with us. However, the same is true of negative emotions. Abuse, conflict, or other traumatic incidents can forge psychic connects with others who continue to drain us of power long after we have parted ways with the person who hurt us. This, ultimately, is the reason that protection magick is so important — it prevents these psychic connections from being made so that when we leave a harmful presence, their energies don't follow us.

That being said, you can cast a cleansing or banishing ritual even if you don't know the source of the psychic attack. Even wearing a simple protective talisman can cause a noticeable lift in your spirits, as it will work immediately to block any negative energies coming at you, whether they are coming from this world or the spirit realm. Most protective and cleansing rituals target all forms of negative energy. Attacks coming from another practitioner and attacks coming from a non-magickal person can be stopped using the same herbs, spells, and rituals.

The same is true for attacks coming from the spirit realm, which can be much harder to identify.

One of the best ways to safeguard ourselves from psychic attacks is to surround ourselves with benevolent people — those who love us will also protect us with their positive energy. The same is true for the spirit realm. The more positive connections you can build with spiritual entities, the more protection you will have from angry spirits or deities. Spiritual entities take many different forms. Just as you are able to pick and choose your physical friends, you can also choose your spiritual friends. Whether you feel particularly drawn to deities, angels, ancestors, plant and animal spirits, or any other being, make sure you put some kind of representation to that spiritual entity on your altar. Leave them regular offerings to draw them to your presence. Think of an offering like sending a text message to a friend — it lets them know that you're thinking of them and that you enjoy their presence in your life. Surround yourself with positive beings in both the physical and the spiritual realm, and the goodwill of your loved ones will be a powerful deterrent to the negative wishes of others.

11

GUARDIAN ANGELS

Angels are some of the most powerful allies we humans have in the spirit realm. Today, angels are most closely correlated with the three major monotheistic religions of Christianity, Judaism, and Islam. For this reason, some practitioners are uncomfortable working with angels as spiritual guides or protectors. But angelic work is really based on spiritual traditions that can be traced back to ancient Hebrew mysticism and that far predate both Christianity and Islam.

People of any and all spiritual backgrounds can work with angels if they choose, and this is because angels, as spirits, are incredibly benevolent. There are spirits called "archangels," or powerful angelic spirits that act like deities or other powerful spirit beings. But there are also spirits called guardian angels. These spirits are no less powerful than archangels, but they are considered "smaller" spirits because they only work with one individual at a time.

Everyone has a guardian angel (sometimes called a "spirit guide"). Your guardian angel is exactly what it sounds like. It's an angel that has taken a vested spiritual interest in your safety and well-being. Should you choose to summon or work with one, you can count on the fact that a guardian angel is waiting to work with and protect you.

If you do choose to summon your guardian angel, you will find yourself with a powerful spiritual friend. Angels are powerful spiritual beings, which is why they are so enduringly popular across so many different spiritual traditions. While the archangels are certainly powerful allies to make, it can be far more comforting to work with a spirit who doesn't work with anyone else. We don't share guardian angels the way that we shared deities, archangels, or other spirits, and this is what makes them particularly unique as spiritual protectors.

When you begin working with angels, you often see lots of information about archangels. These angels have names, sigils, correspondences, and other rituals associated with them. Though they are generally benevolent beings, they should be approached with the same care and respect as a deity.

You can't find the name of your guardian angel in a book of signs, sigils, or correspondences because your guardian angel is unique to you. Of course, when working with your angel, you should be careful and respectful, but you don't have to stand on ceremony with a guardian angel the way that you do with other beings. In this way, working with guardian angels is similar to working with ancestors. These are spirits that have a unique, personal presence in our lives; therefore, we can take a unique, personal approach to their worship.

Opening yourself up to your guardian angel, therefore, does not require a ritual or a summoning. Instead, find a quiet place to meditate and be alone. Spend a few moments in silence and relaxation, allowing your thoughts to clear and your mental chatter to subside. Then send your call out into the universe. Say to your guardian angel that you are ready to bring them into your spiritual practice and that you wish to be reconnected with them. Once you have sent out the call, you should feel a warm and loving presence wash over you. You may have a mental vision of what your guardian angel looks like, or you may gain sudden knowledge of the right symbol or representation of your angel.

There is no need to send your angel away. Having a guardian angel with you at all times is the most powerful protection you can have! As you get to know your angel, set a representation of them on your altar, or make a talisman for them that you can wear around your neck and know your guardian angel is near.

Don't feel discouraged if you don't feel a strong or intimate connection with your angel at first. Like any relationship, it will demand some time for you to learn how best to communicate with your angel and how to feel most comfortable in their presence. It's okay to experiment and to try things out. Your guardian angel will never reject you or leave you; it is often the opposite! In our doubt, anger, or impatience, we can sometimes inadvertently push our guardian angels away. Don't allow your frustration to overwhelm you. Do exactly what feels right, as those feelings might be messages from your angel.

A daily or yearly synchronistic meditation is a great way to check with your guardian angel. Choose a synchronistic time that has excellent numerical significance to you. Synchronistic times happen when both sides of the clock or both numbers in the date are the same number. For example, if you choose to do a daily meditation exercise, choose a time like 10:10, 11:11, 1:01, etc. If you decide to do a yearly meditation, choose a day like 11/11, 12/12, 03/03, etc.

If you choose to do a daily meditation, simply set aside your synchronistic minute for meditating. Nothing fancy is needed. Just pause for one whole minute, and reach out to your guardian angel to send them love and affection. Open yourself up to the love and affection you receive back. It's a simple meditation exercise and a simple ritual, but if you commit to it every day, you will start to feel its positive, energetic effects in every area of your life.

If you choose to do a yearly meditation, then you should set aside that day as a day of solitude, meditation, and spiritual work with your guardian angel. If at all possible, try not to work or commit to any social engagements on that day. Decorate your altar with drawings, gifts, symbols, and objects that connect you to your guardian angel. Spend your day doing meditations, prayers, or ritual workings that give thanks to your guardian angel, and that opens you up to energetically receive the love and affection they hold for you.

If you're still not sure where to start with your guardian angel, try making a talisman for them. One side of the talisman should symbolize you and should be inscribed with your name, birthdate, or another symbol that represents you. The other side should represent your angel. It should be inscribed with the synchronistic number you've chosen for your meditation (if you decide to do so) or another symbol that represents your angel. Don't be hesitant to go with your instincts. The first thing that pops into your head is probably a message from your guardian angel.

If you want to personalize messages and rituals to your guardian angel, you may want to consider using symbols (or even writing letters) using the angelic alphabet. Sometimes called the celestial alphabet, this writing system was invented by medieval practitioners in Europe to better communicate with angels of all kinds in ritual settings. While ceremonial magicians typically use this alphabet to communicate with archangels, it's more than appropriate to use when working with your guardian angel. There are plenty of websites where you can find the symbols of the angelic alphabet and begin using them in ritual communications with your angel.

12

COUNTER-MAGICK

Most protective magick is preventative. Its purpose is to stop negative energies from ever reaching you. However, sometimes negative energies have already gotten through our defenses. When this happens, we need to engage in some counter-magick or spells that are designed not just to banish negative energies but to reflect them back at the source. Like a counter-move in a game of chess, counter-magick is one step up from simple protection charms. Counter-magick is defensive magick. Counter-spells ensure two things — that we are protected and that whatever is attacking us never harms us again. This chapter will outline a few defensive spells to use when you come under psychic attack, and more basic protective spells just aren't getting the job done.

Justice Spell

This spell is most potent in the summer season, especially during the month of July.

Injustices, unfortunately, happen all the time. Whether it manifests as legal, financial, workplace, or healthcare oppression, injustices can do great harm to our well-being. When you are facing some kind of oppression, this is an excellent counter-spell to deflect the powerful negative energies that are surrounding you. For this spell, you will need:

- A block of wood
- A black marker
- A hammer

Using the marker, draw a pentacle on one side of the block of wood. On the other side, write the name of the person for whom you are seeking justice. If that person is you, then write your own name. Hold the hammer in your dominant hand and say these words:

Name this hammer, Justice!

Then sharply tap both sides of the wooden block. Each time, demand that a particular action be taken. For example, if you are in the middle of a legal battle, say something like, *"The judge will make the just decision"* or *"They will see my innocence."* Once you have made your demands, bury the block of wood somewhere on the property where you live.

Social Media

This spell is most potent in the month of July, especially during a waxing moon.

Many of us have online friends — people we mostly interact with through Facebook, Twitter, or even YouTube. Many more of us communicate primarily with our real-life friends through the internet. Social media can be an incredibly positive space — a space where we remain connected to friends and family all over the world. However, it can quickly become a very negative space. We are exposed to so much social energy on social media, and often in a very short amount of time. It's very easy to come under psychic attack on the internet, much easier than many people realize. If you are feeling continuously drained, anxious, or frustrated by your online encounters, this is a simple counter-spell to deflect those negative energies and protect you out in cyberspace. For this spell, you will need the following:

- A cauldron
- Three candles — one red, one orange, and one black
- The tarot cards Justice (Major Arcana VIII) and Strength (Major Arcana XI)

Set the cauldron in the center of your altar. Place the three candles in a triangle in the center of the cauldron. Lay the tarot cards on the altar to the left and the right of the cauldron. You want one card on either side. Now lay your devices (phone, laptop, tablet, etc.) over the cards. Light the candles and say these words:

I call on Justice and Strength to secure my safety on my social media accounts, to bless me with positive connections, and banish those who wish me harm.

Great Powers, protect me from those thieves of my energy who would do me harm on the internet but smile when we are in person.

Let the candles burn all the way down. The walls of the cauldron will protect your electronics from the hot wax.

Technology Protection Spell

This spell is most potent in the summer season, especially during the month of August.

While it's true that we become vulnerable to psychic attacks when using our technology, it's also true that our devices themselves can be the victim of negative energies. August is a transient time in nature, as the wheel of the year changes from summer to fall. This is a slow time of year, a time to give thanks and prepare for the coming colder months (Mankey, 2019). As such, it's a perfect time of year to work protective magick. This spell, most potent when the sun is in Leo, is an excellent counter-spell to protect your technology from viruses, theft, and damage. For this spell, you will need the following:

- Four white candles

Place the four candles in a square on your altar. Place the device you wish to protect in the middle of the square. Visualize the astrological glyph for the sign of Leo hovering over the device and then slowly lowering down until it's absorbed into the technology. Light the four candles, and say these words:

From where I stand,

the sun in the sky shines down and protect this device in hand.

May this current astrology

shield my technology!

Remove the device from the square of candles, but allow the candles to burn all the way down.

Dragon Protection Spell

This spell is most potent in the month of August, especially during a waning moon.

Counter-magick acts as reinforcement when psychic attacks make it through our defenses. Cast this spell to reinforce your protective wards, and to turn your magickal shields into energetic mirrors that reflect negative energies back at their sources. For this spell, you will need the following:

- A Black Candle
- A Small Statue Or Picture Of A Dragon

Light the candle, and say these words:

May the dragon's protection

keep me safe from harm, inside and out.

Hold the statue or picture of the dragon in your hands. Shut your eyes and imagine a circle of protective energy origination from within the dragon's chest and slowly growing outward until you are surrounded by it. Imagine this as a sphere of protective energy, and imagine the dragon perched on the top of the sphere. Hold this image as long as possible. When you let go, place the dragon in the center of your altar. This spell will not only act as a protective ward on its own, but it will also lend strength to any protective spells or guardians you already have in place.

Bless Your Car

This spell is most potent during the fall season, especially during the month of October.

Psychic attacks are actually quite common on the road. Many people hang protective amulets or talismans from their rearview mirrors to keep themselves safe behind the wheel, but sometimes someone's malicious energies break through our primary defenses. This powerful counter-spell will reinforce the defenses you've already erected around your vehicle and keep you safe from energetic attacks while you're driving.

Trace a pentacle with the finger of your dominant hand on each door and window of your car, as well as over the hood and trunk. Imagine these pentacles glowing white, and say these words:

Stars shining bright,

keep this car and all who enter safe within your light.

Magickal shields embedded, infused,

and fully secured.

So mote it be!

Taking Out the Garbage

This spell is most potent in the month of October, especially during a waning moon.

We cast protective spells to keep us safe from harmful people and energies. However, sometimes our lives are entwined with negative people, whether it's a boss, relative, or even the best friend of our partner. We can't completely cut these people out of our lives, but continuous exposure to their nasty energies can wear down our protective spells. This counter-spell is not meant to do any harm. Instead, it's intended to banish this person's influence from your life and instigate natural circumstances that will take you out of their negative path.

Write the name of the person who is giving you trouble, and throw it into the trash, recycling bin, or compost heap. Say these words:

May you come to no harm,

but may you go away,

to somewhere far from me,

to somewhere far from where you now stay.

May you give up that negativity

that doesn't serve you and doesn't serve me.

May you leave me alone.

May you and the unhappiness around you be gone.

So mote it be!

Take out the trash or close the lid on the dumpster or compost bin. The negative influences of this person will be whisked away from your life with the garbage.

13

REVERSAL MAGICK

While counter-magick is meant to step up our defenses when we are in danger, reversal magick is what happens after we've actively been attacked. Rather than breaking or shielding, reversal magick is about banishing negative influences and "reversing" the curse we have been put under.

Four Thieves Vinegar

This spell is most potent in the fall season, especially during the month of November.

The legend of the four thieves is that each of them contributed to a vinegar mixture, drank the potion together, and were, therefore, able to survive a local plague. This spell will help you, like the thieves, to survive whatever plague is raging around you. This could be an illness, but it could also be a "plague" of negativity, conflict, or violence. For this spell, you will need the following:

- Allspice
- Cayenne

- Cinnamon
- Dried peppers
- Peppercorns
- Rosemary
- Sage
- Tarragon
- 1 cup vinegar
- 1 mason jar
- Five garlic cloves

Grind up the herbs and peppercorns with a mortar and pestle. Pour the vinegar into the Mason jar. Chop the garlic cloves in half and put the halves in the jar as well. As you chop each one, call out the names of the five elements (earth, air, fire, water, spirit). Pour the herbs into the Mason jar, screw on the lid, and shake it to "activate" the spell. Store it in a dark area for five days. On the sixth day, take it out of hiding and place it on your altar. This spell is powerful enough to banish negative energies by itself, but for extra power, you can use this vinegar to dress candles or add to potions in other protective spells.

Environmental Guardian Invocation

This spell is most potent in the month of November, especially during a waning moon.

At this point, environmental magick has gone beyond the point of protection or even counter-spells. Some serious reversal magick is required not only to protect the earth from future harm but also allow it to recover from the damage that has already been done. If you are concerned about the future of the planet at large, this invocation is a means for you to add your own voice to the chorus of magickal practitioners casting environmental spells all over the world.

For this spell, choose an earth deity, and place a picture, statue, or representation of them on your altar. Light a blue or white candle to your deity. For extra power, leave them offerings, say a small prayer, or meditate on their image. If you already have an earth deity on your altar, step up your offerings or change them out. Your earth spirits need all the extra power you can give them.

If you don't have an earth deity on your altar, choose one to add to your pantheon. Below are a few earth deities and spirits to help you get started:

Algonquin

Nokomis — earth goddess

Aztec

Atlatonen — earth goddess

Coatlicue — earth goddess

Egypt

Aker — earth god

Geb — earth god

Keb — earth god

Qeb — earth god

Seb — earth god

Tem — earth god

Etruscan

Cel — earth goddess

Celsclan — earth god

Vei — earth goddess

Voltumna — earth god

Finland

Akka- earth goddess

Maanhaltija — earth spirits

Fon

Sagbata — earth god

Greece

Chthonia — earth goddess

Hindu

Prisni — earth goddess

Prithvi — earth goddess

Hittite

Hannahanna — earth goddess

Incan

Mama Pacha — earth goddess

Ireland

Tailtiu — earth goddess

Latvia

Zemes Mate — earth goddess

Lithuania

Zemepatis — earth god

Mayan

God R — earth god

Melanesia

Morufonu — earth god

Norse

Jord — earth goddess

Rome

Tellus — earth goddess

Shinto

Kunitsu-Kami — earth gods

Okuninushi — earth god

Slavic

Mati Syra Zemlya — earth goddess

Tlingit

Hayicanako — earth goddess

Yoruba

Odudua — earth goddess

Zapotec

Mbaz — earth goddess

Human Rights Protection Spell

This spell is most potent in the winter season, especially during the month of December.

Human rights violations happen all around us all the time, in every country around the world. These violations are powerful, traumatic forces that will break through even the best-laid defenses. When these atrocities occur, it's definitely time for some reversal magick to not only banish the forces of oppression but also give the victims the ability to heal and recover.

This reversal spell can be performed by anyone, whether you're simply someone who is concerned about human rights or someone who is directly battling government oppression.

Take a black candle and hold it (unlit) in your hands. Say these words:

There may not be much that

I can do, there may not be much that

I can say, so I give this power to you.

We are not broken; we are not lost.

Protect us all from danger at all costs.

Heal those who have been violated.

Free those who are oppressed. I summon

The power of good to drive all evil away!

Light the candle and place it in a window. Let it burn all the way down.

Peace Candle Spell

This spell is most potent in the month of December, especially during a waxing moon.

Sometimes we cannot seem to rid ourselves of psychically toxic people. Family members, especially, can be challenging to shield ourselves from. This can make the winter holidays a particularly taxing time, as we often find ourselves at parties and other gatherings of family and acquaintances that we would otherwise try to avoid. If you are unable to avoid a coming encounter with someone who has done you great harm, this reversal spell will not only shield you throughout the upcoming meeting but will actually reflect any negative energy thrown at you back onto its source. For this spell, you will need the following:

- Two candles, one white and one blue
- Olive oil
- A piece of white or blue fabric

First, dress each candle with the olive oil. Visualize the coming encounter, whether it's a party, meeting, or outing. Imagine it is a positive and healthy experience for all people involved. Then wrap the candles in the fabric. Put the candles in a dark place, such as a closet or a drawer, for at least two days. On the morning of your encounter, place the candles on your altar and light them. Imagine their flames growing until a warm, protective light surrounds you. Maintain this image for a few moments, and then extinguish the candles. Their protective energy will act as a reflective shield to defend you against any toxic energy that might be sent your way.

Dark Moon Detox

This spell is most potent on a new moon, especially during the winter season.

The dark moon is the opposite of the new moon. It's often described as the time of "lowest power," but that's not entirely true. Instead, the new moon is an energetic pause, a time of stillness before the next moon cycle begins. This quiet space is the perfect time to cast reversal spells. As one cycle ends, you can send out energetic pulses that change the course of the coming cycle. As you banish the negative energies that have plagued you during the previous cycle, you can dedicate the coming moon cycle to growth, healing, and undoing the damage that has been done to you. For this spell, you will need the following:

- One small plate
- Sea salt
- Sage
- One black candle

Sprinkle a healthy layer of sea salt and sage over the surface of the salad plate. Place the black candle in the middle of the plate over the salt and sage. Light the candle. Imagine all heaviness, stuckness, and other harmful or traumatic energies being sucked out of your body, aura, home, and life and into the flame of the black candle. Imagine these negative energies being burned away by the hot wax. Loosen all the muscles in your body and breathe deeply. Release all tension and worry from your mind and body. When you feel totally relaxed, extinguish the candle, or let it burn all the way down. Take steps to initiate the growth and healing power of this spell by cleaning clutter, drinking lots of pure water, or committing to some other physical act of healing.

14

CLEANSE YOUR SPACE

In the aftermath of a psychic attack, negative energies can still cling to our homes or ritual spaces. Regardless of how well your protective measures have held up, it's good to regularly cleanse your ritual space to ensure that no lingering energies are left to interfere with your workings. This chapter will outline a few cleansing rituals to help you clear your space and your life of negative energies to help you start new workings from a fresh, energetic place. Just like physical cleansing rituals (brushing your teeth, taking a shower), spiritual cleansing rituals should be done regularly, whether that's once a year or once a month, to ensure good spiritual hygiene.

Good Vibes Candle

This spell is most potent in the winter season, especially during the month of January.

Place a candle (of any color) in the area you wish to cleanse, whether that's your ritual space, your home, or even your workspace. Close your eyes. Imagine a beam of clear, clean energy or even a stream of clear water running down from the sky and into the candle. Imagine this energy stream passing all the way through the bottom of the candle and deep into the earth. Place your hands around the candle and say these words:

Above and below,

Purifying vibes to stay and to go,

Good, clean energy radiates forth,

And all debris is fully absorbed.

Light the candle to send its cleansing energies out into the space. Extinguish the candle when you leave the area or remain and let the candle burn all the way down for a deep cleanse.

Warm the Soul Incense

This spell is most potent in the winter season, especially during the month of February.

Winter is a time of stillness and introspection. It's a low energy season, and so is the perfect time for clearing and cleansing to prepare for the coming spring. This incense is infused with clearing and purifying energies that will rid your space of lingering negative debris. For this incense, you will need the following:

- Orange zest
- Clove
- Dried lavender
- Spearmint
- Basil
- Rosemary
- Vanilla bean
- Fennel
- Parsley
- Incense charcoal

Light the incense charcoal in a censer. Sprinkle the herbs over the charcoal, and inhale the sweet-smelling smoke. Visualize the smoke spreading through your body, warming you as it goes. Imagine all fears, worries, and depression, leaving your body and leaving your space. Burn this incense anywhere in your home that you feel needs an energetic cleanse.

Banishing Powder

This spell is most potent during the month of February, especially during a waning moon.

This powder is like a super-charged cleansing incense. It is useful for getting rid of particularly nasty energies that just won't go away, especially energies that are deeply rooted in a particular space. For this spell, you will need the following:

- One teaspoon incense ashes
- One teaspoon salt
- One teaspoon garlic powder
- A bowl
- A pin
- Pen and paper

Mix the ashes, salt, and garlic powder together in the bowl using the sharp end of the pin. Imagine a dark cloud gathering around the powder. When you finish mixing, leave the pin in the middle of the powder. On the paper, write or draw whatever it is you wish to banish from your space. Pour the powder and pin over the paper. Imagine whatever is written on the paper being smothered or buried under the powder. Leave this undisturbed on your altar until the situation has been resolved. When the circumstances has been taken care of, burn the paper and scatter the ashes outside.

Ditch Dolls

This spell is most potent during the month of March, especially on March 3.

March 3 is Hinamatsuri, the doll festival celebrated in Japan. This festival comes from an ancient Shinto cleansing ritual. This spell is inspired by contemporary Japanese celebrations of this festival, which include making dolls out of paper or straw and sailing them down a river to remove impurities. For this spell, you will need the following:

- A large leaf for each attribute you wish to release
- Scissors
- Water

Cut each leaf into a roughly human or doll-like shape. Bring your human-shaped leaves to a nearby body of water, whether that is an ocean, lake, or river. Drop the leaves into the water one at a time. For each leaf, say these words:

Begone, out of my life,

and leave a space for something better.

Once you have released all of the negative attributes or energies in your life, turn away and don't look back.

Spring Clearing

This spell is most potent during the spring season, especially during the month of March.

Spring is traditionally a season for cleaning and clearing, especially in early spring. This is the transition from winter, a relatively low-energy season, to summer, which is a very high-energy season. As the pause between winter and summer, spring is the perfect time to reset, refresh, and banish that which is no longer serving you. For this spell, you will need the following:

- A broom
- Stems of lavender
- Stems of rosemary
- Stems of hyssop
- Sea salt
- Spring water
- Candles (any color)
- Olive oil or frankincense oil
- Sage or juniper
- Small bells

First, take a new broom and sweep all of the floors in your living space. If you live in a place with multiple rooms, start in the room attached to the front door and walk clockwise around the house. Bury or scatter all of the physical debris you collect outside.

Next, bind together the stems of lavender, rosemary, and hyssop. Dip them in the salt and water. Use the bundle to sprinkle salt water over each room in the house.

Anoint the candles with olive or frankincense oil. Leave one candle to burn in each room of the house. You can also smudge each room with sage or juniper, but if you choose to do this, remember to cover up your smoke alarm while you're performing the cleanse (and remember to remove the cover once the smoke has dispersed!).

Finally, hang the bells in the corner of every room. As you're hanging the bells, say these words:

I hang these bells, for seasons turn.

I clean with water while candles burn.

I sweep with the broom as the bells ring

and listen for the birds to sing.

Dry Floor Wash Cleaning

This spell is most potent in the month of March, especially during a waning moon.

If there's one particular room in your home or workspace that needs cleaning, this is the perfect spell to get the job done. For this spell, you will need the following:

- Three tablespoons sea salt
- ½ cup dried rosemary, vervain, and sage
- One jar

Mix the herbs and salt together in the jar. Sprinkle the mixture in a circle onto the floor of the room that needs cleansing. Make sure to move in a clockwise direction. Begin in the North, and try to spread it out so that you can make the circle three times. Allow the circle to sit for fifteen minutes.

After fifteen minutes have passed, find a broom and sweep up the mixture. Again, begin in the North and sweep up the circle in a clockwise direction. Once you have swept up the circle, sweep the entire room, preferably moving in a clockwise direction. Burn all of your sweepings in a fire, or scatter them outdoors.

15

PSYCHIC ATTACK

You now know how to recognize a psychic attack, but how do you battle one? What steps do you take when you realize that your defenses aren't strong enough to keep you safe?

The most important point to remember about psychic attacks is that it's tough to know for sure where they're coming from. There may be someone in your daily life that you strongly dislike, but just because you don't like being around someone doesn't necessarily mean that they are negative or that they psychically wish you harm. Though they are called "attacks," psychic attacks rarely leave us feeling wronged or assaulted. The most common symptoms of psychic attacks are feeling drained, chronically fatigued, fuzzy-headed, apathetic, guilty, or depressed. The great news is that you really don't have to know where the attack is coming from to defend yourself against it. However, discerning who is draining our energies is essential for our spiritual wellness. Sometimes we can sense immediately that someone is spiritually toxic for us. Other times, those who are psychically attacking us are (unfortunately) people whom we know and love or people whom we have regular professional contact with.

Knowing who your attacker is can be important if it's someone who is a regular fixture in your life. Your defenses may work for a time, but continued exposure to this person's toxic energy will make you vulnerable to their ill wishes again and again. When your assailant is someone close to you, such as a family member, friend, partner, or co-worker, then it's not enough to defend yourself on the spiritual plane. Some radical lifestyle changes may be necessary to keep you out of harm's way in the future.

Psychic attacks are a form of spiritual bullying and/or abuse. Low-level attacks are often accidental — people don't realize how strong their negative thoughts or feelings can affect others. However, more focused attacks are absolutely intentional. Whether they come from a magickal practitioner or not, the intention is the same. To intimidate you and break your will to do what they have not given you permission to do. This is why psychic attacks often leave us feeling guilty or sluggish. Our energies are being drained away from the things that are important to us. Moreover, they are instead being given to one who wishes us to be spiritually (and emotionally) beholden to them.

The first step in defending yourself from psychic attack, of course, is recognizing that it's happening. Psychic attacks work a bit differently from physical attacks. When someone threatens us with physical violence or says something insulting to our face, we often feel a surge of emotion, whether that emotion is anger, shame, frustration, resentment, fear, or shock. Psychic attacks, on the other hand, leave us feeling emotionally blunt. We feel weak, fuzzy-headed, and sometimes even physically ill, though we can't find any physical cause for our symptoms. If you notice yourself feeling this way, the first step is to reinforce your defenses. Without basic psychic protections in place, we can become vulnerable to the negative energies around us, whether those energies are coming from other people or from the spirit world.

To make an analogy, think of your psychic defenses as your spiritual immune system. You are exposed to a shocking number of pathogens daily, but you rarely get sick because your immune system is capable of neutralizing most of them. However, sometimes we meet a pathogen that is beyond the capabilities of our immune system, and sometimes our immune system is weakened by stress, diet, or other factors. When this happens, we get sick.

In the same way, we are exposed to a great deal of negative energy on a daily basis. If our defenses are strong, we don't even notice them, or we at least aren't influenced by them. If we encounter a particularly strong surge of negativity, however, or if other factors weaken our defenses, then we can come under a psychic attack.

By far, the most obvious form of psychic attack is that which comes at us as an accidental, unconscious expulsion of negative energy from the minds of our fellow human beings. This is particularly true in today's world, where we are psychically linked not only in real life but through the internet. We are exposed to the spiritual energies of potentially hundreds of people every day through social media, e-mail, and messaging apps, and are therefore exposed to the far greater complexity of psychic influences than our ancestors ever were.

However, it's important to remember that most psychic attacks are not deliberate. The other person may not realize the power of the negative energy they harbor within them or how much damage it may have on others. Therefore, it's crucial never to respond to a psychic attack by attacking in kind. You should always be on the defense when it comes to psychic assault because you can't be 100 percent sure who your attacker is, and you can't be sure that your attacker is conscious of the harm they are causing.

The first step when you recognize that you are under attack is to strengthen your defenses. When was the last time you cast a protective spell? When was the last time you renewed the defenses around your altar? Do you have anything defending your home, your vehicle, or your person? Tighten your "security" by filling in any possible gaps. The solution may be as simple as wearing a talisman or amulet under your clothes or carrying a protective crystal in your pocket. Black stones, such as obsidian and tourmaline, are particularly useful for basic protective purposes.

If you strengthen your defenses and you still feel weak, irritable, or emotionally vulnerable, then it may be time for some counter-magick. Counter-spells are fitting for psychic attacks that are actual attacks, instead of an unfortunate encounter with a negative person or spirit. Rather than taking protective measures, actively cast a protective spell that banishes and/or repels negative influences. Spells for banishing, letting go, or cutting ties are all counter-spells that will ward away psychic attacks.

If this spell still doesn't work, it's time for some reversal magick. Reversal spells are the most strongest defensive spells, and they are best for defending against focused attacks that are perpetrated by spirits or by other magickal practitioners. Reversal spells forcibly expel any negative energy from your person or space, but more importantly, they also come with restorative components. Active psychic attacks can leave spiritual and psychological wounds. At this point, it's not enough to simply banish the negative influences — you must also work to heal yourself from the damage that's been done to you.

Cleansing rituals go hand-in-hand with protection. While cleansing spells won't necessarily protect you from psychic attacks, they are important to perform regularly. They are especially important to complete after you have successfully overcome a psychic attack to ensure that no residual energy is left clinging to your aura or your space.

CONCLUSION

Protection from the Evil Eye

The hamsa, the blue eye, and a red horn are all traditional Mediterranean defenses against the evil eye. If you grew up in an Italian, Greek, or Middle Eastern household, you've probably heard a lot about the evil eye, regardless of your family's religious beliefs. But what exactly is the evil eye?

In the simplest terms, the evil eye is jealousy. This emotion is behind most psychic attacks and can cause even the best of us to feel deep resentments toward other people. As such, our ancestors recognized the destructive power of envious thoughts and found various ways to protect themselves from it.

The hamsa and the blue eye are both protective symbols that are specifically designed to keep the wearer safe from the destructive power of the evil eye. However, these symbols will protect you from almost any psychic attack. In the same vein, most defenses that protect against psychic attacks, in general, will also protect you from the evil eye.

Conclusion

It's appropriate to end this book on the evil eye because it speaks to the root nature of the psychic attack. Though we tend to think of demons, possessions, and hauntings when we hear those words, the reality is that psychic attacks almost always come from our fellow humans. A spiritual being practically never casts the evil eye; instead, its harmful gaze usually comes from the people we encounter in the most mundane of situations. Often, psychic attacks come from people whom we live or work with rather than from malicious fellow practitioners or angry ghosts from the spiritual realm.

This book gave you several spells to use throughout the year to keep you safe from a psychic attack. However, the list of spells in this book is far from exhaustive. There are a number of resources out there in print, digital, and oral form that will give you a variety of protective spells, rituals, symbols, and charms to keep you safe from all manner of psychic attack. Certain spiritual protections are more common within different cultural traditions, so feel free to explore your own national or ethnic heritage for strategies on how to protect yourself from negative influences.

Remember that no spell is set in stone. Feel free to edit, experiment, and supplement as best fits your spiritual practice. However, it's also good to remember that spells are written in a certain way for a specific reason. For example, if a spell calls specifically for a black candle or the burning of sage, these aren't arbitrary choices. Black is symbolically the color of protection; hence, many protective rituals will ask you to choose black candles, clothes, stones, or other materials for your workings. If you decide to use a different candle color, make sure that you are choosing not to use black for a specific reason, and make sure that you have a sound spiritual reason for selecting a new color.

The timing of spells is also essential. While any of these spells can be cast at any time, the nature of their energetic influences will be most potent at certain times of the year or during certain phases of the moon. Before doing any ritual work, I would highly suggest keeping the season, the phase of the moon, and the month of the year in mind before you begin working.

In general, it's best not to wait until you've been attacked to protect yourself. Guarding against the evil eye is something you do all the time. You don't wait to put on the charm until after you've been the victim of its negative effects. The same is true for cleansing rituals. While it's important to cleanse after working or after successfully recovering from a psychic attack, cleansing rituals are most effective when done regularly. Spiritual cleansing works the same as physical cleansing. While it's necessary to take a shower after getting dirty, you'll feel the most healthy and clean if you simply take a shower every morning, regardless of how "dirty" you may be.

Finally, when working with protective magick, you should consider who, what, and where you want to protect. Symbols and charms are suitable for protecting your physical and/or spiritual person. You can wear talismans or amulets as jewelry, or you can wear them secretly under your clothes. The blue eye can be purchased as a bracelet, necklace, or even a keychain to serve as both decoration and talisman against the evil eye. Similarly, talismans, amulets, sachets, and protective stones can be given to loved ones as gifts to ensure that they have a small amount of protection as well.

Physical spaces should be protected, as well. Your ritual space, your home, and your workspace are all high-energy places, thus should be maintained both physically and spiritually. Bells and wind chimes protect the home or even a particular room against negative energies. Black candles, cleansing incenses, and other simple rituals can be done to clear or protect your space. The workplace can be the most difficult space for protection magick, as we don't always have the freedom to burn candles or host rituals in our office or company. However, putting a black stone or a protective symbol on your desk can be an easy way to give your workspace some energetic protection. If you have a lanyard or uniform, you can find (or make!) a pin in the form of a protective symbol that you can wear while you are at work. You can even cast protective spells over your name tag, work laptop, or any other item that you specifically associate with work.

In that vein, you can also cast protective magick over your technology. Again, we often forget that cyberspace is a high-energy space and that, if we aren't careful, we can run into some very nasty energies while on the internet. You can decorate your phone or laptop with protective symbols, keep a black stone or burn black candles on the desk where you store your computer, or (carefully) anoint your cell phone with protective oils.

In short, taking protective measures is far from being paranoid or negative. Taking steps to protect yourself spiritually is a sensible and necessary part of any healthy spiritual practice. Being trusting and open is very different from being foolish. You wouldn't take any unnecessary risks with your physical or emotional health. Why, then, expose your spiritual health to dangers that a simple stone or incense will ward off?

I hope that what you have learned in this book will keep you safe from any psychic dangers you may face.

Blessed be!)O(

REFERENCES

Ardinger, B. "Protecting our sacred national spaces." Llewellyn's 2020 spell-a-day almanac. pp. 116. Llewellyn, 2019.

Blackwood, D. "Everyday boundary magic and psychic protection." Llewellyn's 2020 magical almanac. pp. 44–52. Llewellyn, 2019.

Buckland, R. Complete book of witchcraft. Llewellyn, 1986.

Calafia, T. "Protection charm for vulnerable ones." Llewellyn's 2020 spell-a-day almanac. pp. 82–83. Llewellyn, 2019.

Digitalis, R. "Solar citrine as winter light." Llewellyn's 2020 spell-a-day almanac. pp. 18. Llewellyn, 2019.

Fortune, D. Psychic self-defense. Red Wheel/Wiser, 1930.

Freuler, K. "Earth protection spell." Llewellyn's 2020 spell-a-day almanac. pp. 104. Llewellyn, 2019.

Furie, M. "Protection spell jar." Llewellyn's 2020 spell-a-day almanac. pp. 69. Llewellyn, 2019.

References

Kambos, J. "Wipe away negativity." Llewellyn's 2020 spell-a-day almanac. pp. 13. Llewellyn, 2019.

Mankey, A. "Throw the potato away spell." Llewellyn's 2020 spell-a-day almanac. pp. 132. Llewellyn, 2019.

Mankey, J. "Lammas ritual of thanks and protection." Llewellyn's 2020 Sabbats almanac. pp. 262–268. Llewellyn, 2019.

Pesznecker, S. "Woven Protection for the Notorious." Llewellyn's 2020 spell-a-day almanac. pp. 68. Llewellyn, 2019.

Ravenwolf, S. "Earth Goddess Dreaming: A Paper Sachet of She Who Dreams." Llewellyn's 2020 Magical Almanac. pp. 102–107. Llewellyn, 2019.

Whitehurst, T. "Passover meal." Llewellyn's 2020 spell-a-day almanac. pp. 79. Llewellyn, 2019.

Zakroff, L. T. "Eggscellent spell." Llewellyn's 2020 spell-a-day almanac. pp. 80. Llewellyn, 2019.

ABOUT THE AUTHOR

Monique Joiner Siedlak is a writer, witch, and warrior on a mission to awaken people to their greatest potential through the power of storytelling infused with mysticism, modern paganism, and new age spirituality. At the young age of 12, she began rigorously studying the fascinating philosophy of Wicca. By the time she was 20, she was self-initiated into the craft, and hasn't looked back ever since. To this day, she has authored over 40 books pertaining to the magick and mysteries of life.

To find out more about Monique Joiner Siedlak artistically, spiritually, and personally, feel free to visit her **official website.**

www.mojosiedlak.com

- facebook.com/mojosiedlak
- x.com/mojosiedlak
- instagram.com/mojosiedlak
- pinterest.com/mojosiedlak
- bookbub.com/authors/monique-joiner-siedlak

MORE BOOKS BY MONIQUE

African Spirituality Beliefs and Practices

Hoodoo

Seven African Powers: The Orishas

Cooking for the Orishas

Lucumi: The Ways of Santeria

Voodoo of Louisiana

Haitian Vodou

Orishas of Trinidad

Connecting with your Ancestors

Blood Magick

The Orishas

Vodun: West Africa's Spiritual Life

Marie Laveau: Life of a Voodoo Queen

Candomblé: Dancing for the God

Umbanda

Exploring the Rich and Diverse World

Divination Magic for Beginners

Divination with Runes

Divination with Diloggún

Divination with Osteomancy

Divination with the Tarot

Divination with Stones

The Beginner's Guide to Inner Growth

Astral Projection for Beginners

Meditation for Beginners

Reiki for Beginners

Mastering Your Inner Potential

Creative Visualization

Manifesting With the Law of Attraction

Holistic Healing and Energy

Healing Animals with Reiki

Crystal Healing

Communicating with Your Spirit Guides

Empathic Understanding and Enlightenment

Being an Empath Today

Life on Fire

Healing Your Inner Child

Change Your Life

Raising Your Vibe

The Indie Author's Guides

The Indie Author's Guide to Fast Drafting Your Novel

Get a Handle on Life

Get a Handle on Stress

Time Bound

Get a Handle on Anxiety

Get a Handle on Depression

Get a Handle on Procrastination

The Holistic Yoga and Wellness Series

Yoga for Beginners

Yoga for Stress

Yoga for Back Pain

Yoga for Weight Loss

Yoga for Flexibility

Yoga for Advanced Beginners

Yoga for Fitness

Yoga for Runners

Yoga for Energy

Yoga for Your Sex Life

Yoga to Beat Depression and Anxiety

Yoga for Menstruation

Yoga to Detox Your Body

Yoga to Tone Your Body

The DIY Body Care Series

Creating Your Own Body Butter

Creating Your Own Body Scrub

Creating Your Own Body Spray

SUPPORT ME BY LEAVING A REVIEW!

★★★★★

www.ingramcontent.com/pod-product-compliance
Lightning Source LLC
Chambersburg PA
CBHW060838050426
42453CB00008B/746